Build Me A House

Dr. Robert L Robinson

Build Me A House

Dr. Robert L Robinson

Unless otherwise indicated, all Scripture quotations are taken from The King James Version bible (KJV).

Robert Robinson Ministries

To the memory of Lucas my godson,
To Yarnett, my daughter in the Lord: "I heard you singing on that day, and that's what gave me encouragement, Ricky, Tee-Tee, and Marcus. I miss you all and will see you again; rest in Him

To Morris, your endurance and faith is remarkable and encouraging to many; continue to live and walk in that faith, with much love your friend and brother,
Pastor Robby

Table of Contents

Introduction ix

Chapter One
"Build Me a House" 13

Chapter Two
Coming into Order 23

Chapter Three
The First Floor is Finished; Shout about it! 31

Chapter Four
Get Back to Work 45

Chapter Five
The Finished House 53

Chapter Six
The Falling Away and the Remedy 63

Chapter Seven
Seed Killers 73

Chapter Eight
The Baptism of the Local Ministry 83

Chapter Nine
Arise! 91

Books by Dr. Robinson 95

Introduction

Today as we embark on becoming who and what the Church is destined to be, the Lord desires for His house to be built. In Ezra 1:1, the Lord charged Cyrus the king (a Gentile) to build him a house in Jerusalem, which is in Judah. That charge is an unending one and is still being articulated by the Lord today. He desires a house to be built. Since the call is from the Lord, there is but one agenda, and it's His, and anything outside of His agenda has no significance. All of our visions, ideas, hopes, goals, and dreams must acknowledge the will of the Father.

What type of house shall this be? The house that the Lord desires shall be a corporate house comprised of His believers who are created in His image. It is a many-membered house made up of three sections. The first section of the House is the foundation, which represents the individual (it's personal). The second section of the house is the framing. The framing represents the local church. The third section of the house is the corporate body, which is a complete body. The third section is the full finished house, the finished product.

If the first section is not built properly, then the second and third section will not be proper. This concept is geared towards the local church, and to build a local church, individuals are needed first, then the framing or structuring of those individuals, and then there is the finished product. The finished products of God are those people who are made and walk in His image (Gen. 1:26). The finished products are those who are of His faith (the God kind of faith), and a house full of the faithful (God's faith working within that house). The finished house is a corporate body of Christ, a corporate houseman or a one-man house (Ezra 3:1), a many membered house (1 Cor. 12:14).

Many today have become bewildered and preoccupied, silent, tired, frustrated, and faithless. We have lost our focus and settled in Babylon. How did we end up here? We ended up in Babylon because of idol worship; we lost our focus and placed emphasis on things that did not either pertain to or glorify God. It has hindered us immensely and hindered the House of the Lord from being built. But the Lord is calling; His agenda and His vision are being revealed to His Body. He wants a place to live in and be glorified in His house that shall be built in the midst of His people.

In Amos 9:11 the Lord stated that He would raise the tabernacle of David, which is fallen, and close up the breaches. He would cause the ruins to rise and be built as it was during the days of Old. A broken focus has caused us to become a fallen, divided, exposed, naked place, but God is going to restore that place and restore a people. Those people shall possess that place and those are a people who are called by His great name.

Song of Solomon 2:10
My beloved spake, and said unto me, Rise up, my love, my fair one, and come away.

The Lord is calling for His Love (the church) to arise and come away. He is calling for us to arise and come and build.

Acts 3:6
Then Peter said, Silver and gold have I none; but such as I have give I thee: In the name of Jesus Christ of Nazareth rise up and walk.

Prophetically, Peter who represents the Lord goes to a man who was crippled for over forty years. This man represents a downtrodden church or ministry that has been in the position of begging for over 40 years. The man represents a broken focus, a broken ministry, and a broken life. Peter tells the man that silver and gold (man's silver and gold, man's idols) he does not have. Why doesn't Peter have silver and gold? Because before we can have houses and riches, we must get full of God and empty of everything else. The only thing that we will have to give is Jesus Christ, and that is the "but such as I have give I thee." The apostle Peter tells the man in the name of Jesus rise up and walk. God is pulling on His church right now to leave the seat of do-nothing and walk in the name of Jesus. The Lord is pulling us up out of the seat of do-nothing and into a place where we become His house.

The Holy Spirit moved me to write this book after numerous weeks of teaching out of the book of Ezra. At the time I was finished teaching, tragedy hit my life like nothing that I could ever imagine. A dear friend of mine lost his family. I was blown away, and because of that tragedy this book became an unfinished thing. I became one who lost focus. I became like the crippled man at the gate and settled in that slumped position for what seemed like years. The Holy Spirit would move me to grasps the pen and continue to write; however, I, like those in Haggai 1:2, said it is not time yet. The longer I procrastinated, the more silent the words of the Lord became in my ears.

Finally, I had to make a decision: either I can become a mountain of dry, dead bones like Ezekiel saw and die an unfinished house, or I can resume my work and become a finished thing. This was a very important decision in my life because my future and the future of my family and church depended on the decision that I would make. I am glad that I made the right decision. Now I can truly say that there is no agenda in my life but God's agenda; everything else is secondary. I must become the very thing the Lord has in His mind concerning me and so do you. We must become His house, which is a built-settled Temple that houses His image.

I love you and pray that as you read these pages, the Holy Spirit reveals to you what the Father is calling out of you this day.

R.L. Robinson

Chapter One

"Build Me a House"

Ezra 1:1-2
Now in the first year of Cyrus king of Persia, that the word of the Lord by the mouth of Jeremiah might be fulfilled, the Lord stirred up the spirit of Cyrus king of Persia, that he made a proclamation throughout all his kingdom, and put it also in writing, saying, Thus saith Cyrus king of Persia, The LORD God of heaven hath given me all the kingdoms of the earth; and he hath charged me to build him an house at Jerusalem, which is in Judah.

In 538 BC, it was the first year that Cyrus king of Persia, reigned over Babylon, the city that was captured by Persia. In that year Cyrus received a Word from the Lord to build the Lord a house. The Lord wanted His house to be built. Isaiah prophesied in Isaiah 44:28 some 150 years before that he (Cyrus) would be the Lord's shepherd and shall perform all of His pleasure and even Jerusalem shall be built along with the temple and the foundations shall be laid. Isn't this ironic? Cyrus was spoken of some 150 years before he was king; his life was already ordered by the Lord (Ps. 37:23). If the Lord God spoke that of Cyrus before he was born, it makes one wonder what God has spoken of us before we were born. Our destiny exists in what God has spoken over the life of the believer before he or she had a body. When did he speak it? He spoke it over you before the foundation of the world. At the timing of the Lord, He was ready for Cyrus, and today He is calling for Cyrus to come and proclaim the prophetic Word of the Lord.

Jer. 29:10-11
For thus saith the Lord, That after seventy years be accomplished at Babylon I will visit you, and perform my good word toward you, in causing you to return to this place.

The words of the prophet Jeremiah are about to be fulfilled. Jeremiah prophesied that the Lord would visit His people after 70 years of captivity, perform his good word towards them, and cause them to return to this place. The 70 years represents a time of captivity while living in Babylon. The word *Babylon* is the Hebrew word *Babel* (baw-bel'), which means "confusion." Its root word means, "an overflowing," so *Babylon* means a place of an overflowing confusion. After the time of living in the place of an overflowing confusion that has held you captive, the Lord would do three things: visit you, perform His good word toward you, and cause you to return to this place. Let us look at the word *visit*. The word *visit* is the Hebrew word *paqad* (paw-kad). It means "to go to any person or thing." The next word to look at is the word *perform*. It is the Hebrew word *quwn*, which means "to cause to come forth or to exist, to raise up any one. The Lord is saying, "At the end of your overflowing confusion, I will go to you and cause my good word to come forth and exist." That good word shall cause you to return to this place. Where is "this place?" This place is called Jerusalem. The word *Jerusalem* is divided into two words, *Yeru* and *shalem*. *Yeru* is the Hebrew word that means "the foundation of." The Hebrew word *Shalem* means "peace." Jerusalem means "The foundation of Peace." The foundation of peace is the place *of* God and also a place *in* God. The Lord wants to come to our ministries and also to us individuals who have lived in Babylon for a while and cause His good word to exist in the midst of His people. That good word will cause His people to go up to the place of Peace. In him is that place that is called the Place of Peace or the Place of Certainty.

How does one end up in Babylon? One ends up in Babylon because of idol worship. The Lord is bringing us from that place (a city) of an overflowing confusion. He is taking us through the process of getting rid of the silver and the gold. He is going to perform His Good Word towards us. We are learning to live in the "but such as I have give I unto thee" of God. He is visiting us or depositing some things in His people. He is performing his good word in us causing us to rise up and return. Where are we returning? We are returning to Jerusalem, which is the foundation of peace, the place of peace, the place of certainty in Him.

14

We are returning to the place of who we are supposed to be a place of His image after His likeness: A place where He is forming or building His house!

A Stirring

According to Ezra 1:1, the Lord stirred up the spirit of Cyrus. To start building His house will take a stirring of the spirit. The prophetic functions in three stages:

1. First there must be a spoken word.
2. Second, the recipient of the prophetic word must then prepare for what was spoken.
3. The third stage of the prophetic is all that was prophesied is now manifested and all that was prophesied comes into its fullness.

In Ezra 1:1, the Babylonian captivity was, over and now God was beginning to speak. The Lord stirred up the spirit of the King. This action represents a fresh Word coming into a particular house. A Fresh Word will come through a leader who has been stirred. The leaders of today definitely need a stirring. The word *stirred* is the Hebrew word *'uwr* (oor). It refers to the idea of opening the eyes to be made awake. The root word means "to be made naked." The word *stirred* means "to open the naked or the opening up of the naked eye." The naked eye is the spiritual eye (Eph. 1:18). This is the type of vision the leader must have, a naked eye that sees what the Lord is calling for.

The first section of the house must be sought. This seeking is called vision. As previously stated, the first section of the house deals with an individual, "the believer." The believer must be stirred; your eyes (spiritual eyes) must be opened so that one can see what God is saying to the House. The Holy Spirit circumcises our eyes and our ears. Then that same surgical process takes place in the believer that gets up under the vision so that we can all see the same thing!

Leadership inspires to the point that the Holy Spirit will write on the walls of the heart. After Cyrus' spiritual eyes were opened, he began to proclaim and write or inscribe the message. Where did he write it? It was inscribed in the hearts of the people (Heb. 8:10). The leader must proclaim the vision of the Lord. When a leader who is functioning in the prophetic proclaims the Word of the Lord, the voice of that leader becomes the pen of the Holy Spirit. As we proclaim the vision of God, our proclamation of the vision becomes the pen of the Holy Spirit and the proclamation of that vision is "written" in the hearts of the people. The writing in the heart is the work of the Holy Spirit. The Holy Spirit shall inscribe the message, the Word, into the Hearts of the people, and He shall be to us our God, and we shall become to Him a People. The inscribed word will cause His Church to go from what God has spoken into a time of preparation to become what God has said.

The Lord charged Cyrus. The charging of the Lord is the decreeing of the Lord. The Lord decreed it and Cyrus agreed with it. It was no time to attempt to bargain with the Lord; it is not my will but thy will be done. The Lord charged Cyrus, and Cyrus charged or commanded the people to build God a house. The charge is going forth now; God is charging His leaders to charge His people to build Him a house.

A Call to Sacrifice

> Ezra 1:3
> *Who is there among you of all his people? his God be with him,*
> *and let him go up to Jerusalem, which is in Judah, and build the*
> *house of the LORD God of Israel, (he is the God,) which is in*
> *Jerusalem.*

The charge to build the house of the Lord is one that calls for sacrifice. Jerusalem is the city while Judah is the territory. The gate of a city is dependent upon the strength of the city; the strength of the city is dependent upon the strength of the territory! The house was to be built at Jerusalem, which is in Judah. Jerusalem, the city of Peace; the House of God; the place of certainty. Where is Jerusalem? Jerusalem is in the province of Judah. The word *Judah* means "praise", so where is the place of peace? The place of peace is in the Praise. The Praise is where the Lord lives (Psalms 22:3). Learn to praise God so that you can have the Peace and certainty of God. It is time to get ready to take a trip up to Jerusalem, which is in Judah.

Verse 3 asks a question, Who is there among all of his people? In other words, Who are those that are left over? And his God be with him, and let him "go up" to the city of peace which is in the praises of God and build the house (a dwelling place in the midst of His people) of the Lord God of Israel. *Go up* is the Hebrew word *alah* (aw-law'), which means "to ascend." This word is connected with the sacrificial term *olah* in the Hebrew, which means, "what goes up in smoke." Those who will go up are those who are willing to sacrifice, a living sacrifice, which is a sweet savour offering (Phil. 2:8). The sacrifice was placed on the altar, and the smoke ascended, or *alah,* before the presence (face) of God. "To go up" means "to ascend" into the presence (face) of the Lord.

Where are we ascending to in the Spirit? What are we offering upon the altar? Where are we sacrificing? We are sacrificing in Jerusalem, Judah; we are going to the city of peace in the praises of God to give Him ourselves. What we are is what we offer, for what comes out of you goes up as smoke before Him. "Let him ascend or offer up a sacrifice at the place of peace which is in the praises."

True sacrifice calls for the heart first. In Acts 3:6, "*Then Peter said, Silver and gold have I none; but such as I have give I thee: In the name of Jesus Christ of Nazareth rise up and walk.*" The heart is first, and I am so empty of the silver and the gold (mentality) that all I am full of is Him and all that I have is Him to offer to you. Once the heart is given, then all that I have belongs to Him. Though we might have silver and gold, it is no longer our god. We then live in the "and such as I have give I thee." ALL THAT I HAVE BELONGS TO HIM. There is but "one Lord, one faith and one baptism" (Eph. 4:5). The "One Lord" means He is all and has all; "one faith" means He is certain, He is working in and through me; "one baptism" means I am completely submerged in Him.

Ezra 1:4
And whosoever remaineth in any place where he sojourneth, let the men of his place help him with silver, and with gold, and with goods, and with beasts, beside the freewill offering for the house of God that is in Jerusalem.

The word *remaineth* is the Hebrew word *sha'ar* (shaw-ar'). The root word means "to swell up becoming stationary, the rest." *Remain* means "to prop up, to become stationary, to rest." The word *sojourneth* is the Hebrew word *guwr* (goor), which means "to turn aside from the road" (for a lodging or any other purpose), i.e., "sojourn" (as a guest), "a temporary stay." The process of the people of God going up to Jerusalem for sacrificing in the presence of God requires that we stay there just until His process is through. Let Him build Himself within you and His Church. Those who remained are survivors.

The survivors are those who have learned how to rest in the position of sacrifice. A survivor is known as an overcomer.

1 John 2:13-14
I write unto you, fathers, because ye have known him that is from the beginning. I write unto you, young men, because ye have overcome the wicked one. I write unto you, little children, because ye have known the Father. I have written unto you, fathers, because ye have known him that is from the beginning. I have written unto you, young men, because ye are strong, and the word of God abideth in you, and ye have overcome the wicked one.

Rev. 3:21
To him that overcometh will I grant to sit with me in my throne, even as I also overcame, and am set down with my Father in his throne.

Rev. 12:11
And they overcame him by the blood of the Lamb, and by the word of their testimony; and they loved not their lives unto the death.

The word *overcome* is the Greek word *nikao* (nik-ah'-o), which expresses the means of success through conquering to prevail. It also means "to get the victory." It is the death, burial, and resurrection. The death represents death to the flesh; the burial represents that whatever is dead should be buried (getting rid of the dead issues in your life, Matt. 8:22); and then the resurrection represents God's day, His time; He breathes us in, then breathes us out (Hosea 6:1).

The survivors were to help finance the project in any way possible. The overcomers, who have experienced the death, burial, and resurrection process of God, had the spirit of excellence, and nothing is too great or too expensive for the work of the ministry! It's time to become the Living Sacrifice (Rom. 12:1). Let the fire upon the altar burn in order to create

"SMOKE." "Let us go up" to the place of certainty, the place of peace in the land of praise as we sacrifice everything. The Old Man had silver and gold; however, that old man is dead. Now the new man has silver and gold, but it is The Lord's, not man's. It is His Gold and His silver, which is able to finance the House of God. However, before we can give money, we must give Him our hearts.

Who is there among you willing to sacrifice and go to Jerusalem (city of Peace, place of peace, place of Certainty), which is in Judah (Praise)? Those who have remained (in the presence of God) while everything around them was difficult and through sojourning (passing through) in those difficult times still boldly take what the Lord has given them, which is their talents and gifts, and build house of the Lord with those gifts and talents.

> *Ezra 1:5*
> *Then rose up the chief of the fathers of Judah and Benjamin, and the priests, and the Levites, with all them whose spirit God had raised, to go up to build the house of the LORD which is in Jerusalem.*

The chief of the fathers of Judah and Benjamin and the priest were the Leaders of Judah (Praises) and Benjamin (sons of the right hand). The fathers of Benjamin were those who walked in authority. *Benjamin* is divided in two words *ben*, which means "son of" and *Jamin*, which means "right hand." Those are the people who walked in total authority. The Priests represent the whole house of faith (Rev. 1:6; 5:10), and then there were the Levites who served within the ministry. *"With all them whose spirit God had raised"* means God has opened up their naked (spiritual) eye, *"The eyes of your understanding being enlightened; that ye may know what is the hope of his calling, and what the riches of the glory of his inheritance in the saints"* (Eph. 1: 18). These were able to see vision. They did not see men as trees (Mark 8:24) but saw men as precious things. The people of God who possess the spirit of revelation and vision who also sacrificed and gave God their hearts (Rom. 12:12) up in Jerusalem, which is in Judah, are in the process of building and becoming the very House of God.

> *Ezra 1:6*
> *And all they that were about them strengthened their hands with*

vessels of silver, with gold, with goods, and with beasts, and with precious things, beside all that was willingly offered.

The word *about* is the Hebrew word *cabiyb* (saw-beeb'). It means "to revolve, surround or border" or "circle around." They surrounded them and strengthened (fastened) their hands, meaning those that were around those who were going up to Jerusalem grabbed their silver and goods and gave to the project of the Lord. Who are those that are mentioned? They are a people for His name, they are those who rose up to build, they are those who were stirred, and they are those who have become a sacrifice. If we get involved with the work of the ministry, then those who see the work will strengthen their hands to whatever they have in order to finance the kingdom (Luke 6:38). They who surrounded "them" heard the proclamation and could not help but become part of the work that was going on. They (those who surrounded the Israelites), the believers, seized (grabbed) their silver, gold, goods, beasts and "Precious things." The Precious Things prophetically speak of those who have been converted because of the proclamation which went out from the king Cyrus they are those who heard the gospel being declared and proclaimed.

> Acts 4:33-35
> *And with great power gave the apostles witness of the resurrection of the Lord Jesus: and great grace was upon them all. Neither was there any among them that lacked: for as many as were possessors of lands or houses sold them, and brought the prices of the things that were sold, And laid them down at the apostles' feet: and distribution was made unto every man according as he had need.*

The apostles preached the resurrection of the Lord Jesus; they proclaimed Him and those who were around gave of their precious things. The precious things represented their Hearts. They got saved. When the people become the habitation of God, it creates an atmosphere because the hearts of those who surround the people of God are changed.

> Ezra 1:7
> *Also Cyrus the king brought forth the vessels of the house of the Lord, which Nebuchadnezzar had brought forth out of Jerusalem, and had put them in the house of his gods.*

Just as the Lord stirred the Spirit of Cyrus, He intends on stirring the Spirit of the Pastor, for the people cannot be stirred until the leader is stirred. Cyrus brought forth the vessels of the house of the Lord, which was previously taken out by Nebuchadnezzar. Now the pastor king Cyrus is restoring the vessels; the wounded hearts of the overcomers and survivors of that time of captivity are being restored back to the temple; those who have been sitting by the sidelines and not really getting involved with ministry because of circumstances are being restored back to the temple. God's Cyrus, which can be a man or woman of God, is now beginning to through the Holy Spirit speak a Word that will restore all that has been taken away by the enemy Nebuchadnezzar. There is now a word from the Lord that will restore the people of God. Some overcomers and survivors have been troubled, perplexed, persecuted, cast down; however, we have moved into a new season, and the leaders today (the Cyrus's) will have a Word of prophecy (a proclamation) that will heal, deliver, and set free that the excellency of the power may be of God and not of us. The Spirit of Restoration and Vision must be evident in the people before a ministry or person can take on any task.

> *Joel 1:4*
> *That which the palmerworm hath left hath the locust eaten; and that which the locust hath left hath the cankerworm eaten; and that which the cankerworm hath left hath the caterpillar eaten.*

> *Joel 2: 25-26*
> *And I will restore to you the years that the locust hath eaten, the cankerworm, and the caterpillar, and the palmerworm, my great army which I sent among you. And ye shall eat in plenty, and be satisfied, and praise the name of the LORD your God, that hath dealt wondrously with you: and my people shall never be ashamed.*

> *John 10:10*
> *The thief cometh not, but for to steal, and to kill, and to destroy: I am come that they might have life, and that they might have it more abundantly.*

The Spirit of Restoration

The word *restore* in Joel 2:25 is the Hebrew word *shalam* (shaw-lam'). It means, "to be safe in mind, body, or estate." John 10:10 reads, "I am come," which is in the present tense. Christ is come right now to reconnect us to what was spoken by the Father. The thief (idol worship) has robbed us; however I AM COME that we might have *zoe* (dzo-ay) "life," that we might have it more abundantly, *perissos* (per-is-sos'), the root means "with respect to;" this word means superabundant (in quantity) or superior (in quality). So the life that the Lord wants to restore unto His people is one that is in respect to a superior and excessive one. Cyrus restored the goblets and everything that was taken out of the first temple by Nebuchadnezzar. Nebuchadnezzar has come again to the people of God; however, that which the enemy has stolen from the believer, the local church, and the corporate body is now being restored. Christ is come, and He is doing it in the now. The Lord is restoring His name within His people. Everything that His name represents is being restored within His people and His Church. The Spirit of restoration is here. God not only wants to restore the stolen things, but he wants to restore His name within a people who have gone up to sacrifice in Jerusalem, which is in Judah!

Chapter Two

Coming into Order

Ezra 1:8
Even those did Cyrus king of Persia bring forth by the hand of
Mithredath the treasurer, and numbered them unto Sheshbazzar,
the prince of Judah.

Ezra 1:8 represents the 2nd stage of how a prophetic Word operates. At this stage we are at the second level, which is the preparing for what has been prophesied. God said He wants a House; we must prepare (get in order) to build that House. The vessels also were brought forth "By the Hand" of Mithredath. "By the hand" reveals a Five Fold Ministry (Eph. 4:11-16) concept. This thing has got to be started by the Hand of the Lord (a coming into Order). The King (Cyrus) typifies God giving to the Hand of Mithredath (treasurer). This is a Matthew 14:19 Concept. Jesus gave the Bread and Fishes (Word) to His disciples, and the disciples gave it to the people. The King supplied the gold. The King gave it to the treasurer, and the treasurer gave the gold and silver to Sheshbazzar (Zerubbabel). God will supply the need; however the Church today must be GOOD STEWARDS of God's Money. In the second chapter of Ezra there is to be noticed how the Church is coming into God's order. God calls for:

1. Leadership (Ezra 2:2)
2. The Families (Churches) (Ezra 2:2-20)
3. The Cities (Ezra 2:21-35)
4. The Priests (Ezra 2:36-39)
5. The Levites (Ezra 2:40-42) (74 returned) 3 Orders within the Levites returned
   a. Sons of Jeshua (Jehovah is Salvation)

  b. Sons of Kadmiel (Before or in front of God)

  c. Hodaviah (His Glory)

 6. The Singers 128 (one order returned) (Ezra 2:41)

  a. Sons of Asaph (or members of the choir of Asaph)

 7. The Porters or Doorkeepers: 139 (6 orders returned) (Ezra 2:42)

  a. Sons of Shallum (requital or restitution)

  b. Sons of Ater (left handed)

  c. Sons of Talmon (oppression, outcast)

  d. Sons of Akkub (Subtle, to take by the heel)

  e. Sons of Hatita (my sin removed, a digging)

  f. Sons of Shobai (my captives)

 8. Nethinim (the temple servants) (Ezra 2:43-48)

Ezra 2:59-60
And these were they which went up from Telmelah, Telharsa, Cherub, Addan, and Immer: but they could not show their father's house, and their seed, whether they were of Israel: The children of Delaiah, the children of Tobiah, the children of Nekoda, six hundred fifty and two.

In Ezra 2:59-60, there were unconfirmed claims of Israelite Birth. The importance of family records was two-fold: for settling claims to property and for ensuring that the restored community had an unbroken descent from the original Israel. But it was not pressed beyond this point: the unsuccessful claimants were not sent back but evidently given provisionally the same standing as the circumcised foreigners. These could not show their father's house, and their seed, whether they were of Israel or not. This number was 652. There will be many that come to the House of the Lord without a background. Many of those will not know who they are, but we have to let them in and restore them to the kingdom. This is all a part of God's order.

The Church had everything it needed:
1. 7337 slaves (servants) and handmaids
2. 200 singing men and women (a distinct group from verse 41)
3. 736 Horses
4. 245 Mules
5. 435 Camels
6. 6720 Asses

The Money was provided
And some of the chiefs (heads) of the fathers offered freely for the House of God to set it up in His place (Ezra 2:68); they gave:
1. 61000 drams of Gold (68,625 pounds)
2. 5000 pounds of silver (30,000 pounds)
3. 100 Priests Garments

So all dwelt in their cities (Local Church). Every area within the Local Church must come into order so that the whole ministry can go up to Jerusalem to build God a House. If the areas within the local ministry do not come up, there will be no going up to Jerusalem, which is in Judah. The Lord has been trying to get His House built for years. There are no more excuses; everything has been provided. He has spoken, but the people have not responded. In this day and time, it will be God's agenda and His alone. Nothing in our personal lives will prosper until we build the House of the Lord first. Remember, this house is in three sections. The first section is an individual thing (God is dealing with you). The second section is the framing of that house. This represents the local ministry (He deals with the Local Church). The third section is the finished product, a full measured corporate body of Christ (God deals with the corporate body). He has provided everything that is needed to build His house.

The Seventh Day

> *Ezra 3:1-3*
> *And when the seventh month was come, and the children of Israel were in the cities, the people gathered themselves together as one man to Jerusalem.*

At this point in the book of Ezra, we are still in the second stage of the prophetic Word. However, we are getting ready to enter into the 3rd realm (manifestation). This is the 7th month. This is a time of moving. The Children of Israel left Babylon and went back to Jerusalem (the place of Peace, the place of Certainty), which is in Judah (Praise). This distance was about 900 traveling miles, which should have taken approximately four months to travel, according to Ezra 7:8-9. The journey covered 900 miles and lasted four months from Nisan 1 (Mar- April) to Ab 1 (July-Aug) 458 BC. The number 4 is the number for leadership and direction. It was the seventh month:

1. The 7th day was blessed and sanctified (Gen. 2:3)
2. The Ark rested in the 7th month (Gen. 8:4)
3. The 7th day is the Sabbath (rest) (Ex. 20:10)
4. The man asked Jesus to heal his son or the son would die. Jesus spoke the Word and the man believed. On his way back home he met some servants who told the man that his son was healed. The man asked the servants what time did it happen and they told him it was the 7th (seventh) hour, (John 4:52)
5. The opening of the 7th seal produced a silence (Rev. 8:1)
6. There were Seven Feast Days
7. The seventh month, Day, and Hour all speak of the rest of God, the rest in God.

It is important to remember that in order to move, expand, and grow, there must be alignment and order in all three realms individually, in the local church, and in the corporate Body. Here in Ezra, they did not just move when they got ready but they waited for the Seventh Month (Lev. 23:23-34). The seventh month also equals the 7th day. The 7th day is the Day of God (Heb. 4:4). The Seventh month and the seventh Day are a month and a Day of God's Faith (certainty). The Seventh month celebrations are (taken from my book entitled "A Time to Work[1]" :

1. The Feast of the Trumpets. The Feast of Trumpets represents a season of prophetic utterance. The Day of Trumpets fell on the first day of the seventh month.
2. The Day of Atonement. The Day of Atonement was observed on the tenth day of the seventh month. This represented a time of cleansing, preparation, breaking, humbling, stripping, a crying out to God, a cry and prayer of repentance for the sins that were committed against God and each other (our brothers and sisters). The seventh month is the Sabbath month, the month of rest (Heb. 4:1-10).
3. The Feast of Tabernacles (Ingathering). The Feast of Tabernacles was simply called the Feast. Its observance combined the Ingathering of the labor of the field (Ex. 22:16). This feast fell five days after the Day

---

[1] Robert L. Robinson, "A Time to Work" (Providence, RI: FDC Publishing House 1994) Pg. 16.

of Atonement and lasted for seven days. This feast started on the 15th day of the month. This Feast represents a World Harvest.

The Feast Days:
1. The Feast of the Passover
2. The Feast of Unleavened Bread,
3. The Feast of the Firstfruits
These reveals what Christ has done for us through His death.

4. The Feast of Pentecost
This reveals the Holy Ghost experience.

5. The Feast of Trumpets
6. The Day of Atonement
7. The Feast of Tabernacles
Deal with a prophetic instruction for the church. Before anything can happen, there first must be a prophetic proclamation, an alarming of the trumpet. Once we are spoken to, then we must become one with God, his Way and His Plan. There must be a feast of Trumpets and a Day of Atonement and if we prayerfully acknowledge those two feast days, they will lead us into the third feast (Tabernacle or Ingathering), which is the result of the preceding two days. During the third feast, we will see a world harvest.

It was the 7th month, which was a time for celebration. In this month (the 7th month) the people then gathered themselves together as one man. This one man is a Corporate Houseman. He is:
1. One man with many members
2. The infilling and indwelling of every believer
3. He who is housed within the walls of His tabernacle (Eph. 2:21; 4:16)
4. The one set of bones who became an exceeding great army (Ezek. 37:10)
5. He is the exceeding great army which is a person (Ezek. 37:10)
6. The very breath of His Father

27

7. The very breath of His people

The people gathered themselves together and became the One Man, the very Corporate Body of Christ. They became One Man in the Seventh month.

> *Ezra 3:2*
> *Then stood up Jeshua the son of Jozadak, and his brethren the priests, and Zerubbabel the son of Shealtiel, and his brethren, and builded the altar of the God of Israel, to offer burnt offerings thereon, as it is written in the law of Moses the man of God.*

The leadership in this passage is functioning as one man in rightful positions. The Leaders who are supposed to be first partakers stood up. They "stood up" (Rise up and build). Jeshua and Zerubbabel represent a king-priest ministry: *And hath made us kings and priests unto God and his Father; to him be glory and dominion for ever and ever. Amen* (Rev. 1:6). It was this ministry (king-priest) that built an altar. The Altar was the very first thing that was built. The Greek word for *altar* is *thusiasterion* (thoo-see-as-tay'-ree-on), which means "a place of sacrifice." The altar was a place of sacrifice where everything of necessity for worship was placed. The altar today is not only the heart of man but also the center of any ministry. The type of local ministry depends on the type of altar that is in the center of that ministry. If there is an altar that is cold with absolutely no fire, then that is the type of ministry or image of ministry that will be portrayed. However, if one has an altar that is lit with the fire of the Holy Spirit, then one will have a ministry that will portray that fire: *"The fire shall ever be burning upon the altar; it shall never go out"* (Lev. 6:13). Remember, the House that God wants built is a three-sectioned house. The first section has an altar that is upon the heart of the believer. The second section has an altar that is in the center of the local church. The third section has an altar, the altar of the Lord, which is at the center of the Body of Christ. The flame on all three altars (which are ultimately the same altar) burns continuously with the flames of the Holy Ghost.

> *Ezra 3:3*
> *And they set the altar upon his bases; for fear was upon them because of the people of those countries: and they offered burnt offerings thereon unto the LORD, even burnt offerings morning and evening.*

28

The word *set* is the Hebrew word *kuwn* (koon) which means "to be erect, to stand perpendicular, and to set up." It means literally to establish, fix, prepare, and apply. The altar is the place of appointment, prosperity and certainty. The altar was erected, stood perpendicular. It was reared upon its bases or former place. The base of the altar was buried beneath rubble and trash; however, the king-priest ministry went and dug up that base and restored it into its former place. There are some things that must be dug up. Some things will not ever change. This was not a new altar, for there is only one altar. It was important that they begin the building project properly. The first thing they did was restore the altar, meaning they had to establish the right relationship as a matter of first priority. In spite of the fear the people had because of their surroundings, their threats, and pressures of the world, conditions and circumstances demand our return to God's altar, that He may meet with us there (Ex. 29:43).

This took place in the 7th month (7th day). This is the 7th day from Adam and the 3rd Day from Jesus. It is a time of coming into order (a coming together). Both days are a time of resurrection and restoration. The Sons of Israel (Leaders) are in their cities (local churches) and are gathering (Psa. 50:5) unto Jerusalem as one man (this is Jesus Christ and His Brethren Heb. 2:6-13) is standing up in a king-priest ministry. That ministry found the altar and put it back in its place. Fear was upon the people because of their surroundings; however; it was what the people needed to keep them at the very altar of the Lord. This has to take place in the 7th month. It is the 7th month, the 7th day of God, the 3rd Day the day of resurrection. It is time to go and find those things that we have lost. We have lost relationships with each other. We have lost souls, children, and hearts. This is the day of God where His faith working within His Church is functioning. While the anointing is flowing in His day, it is time to go (Heb. 6:1), move, do, perform, build, pull out, pull up, and restore while it is in His day. The faith of God (His certainty) that worketh in you is needed in this day. Release the faith of God that is working in you into the very realm of impossibility.

29

Chapter Three

The first floor is finished; shout about it!

Ezra 3:6
From the first day of the seventh month began they to offer burnt
offerings unto the Lord. But the foundation of the temple of the
Lord was not yet laid.

The Church (Body of Christ) must understand that it is the seventh
month. The seventh month represents the rest of God: rest in God, rest in
the faith or certainty of God. It is also a time to offer up (sacrificially) the
very best that we have. In Ezra 3:6 the foundation of the temple was not
yet laid; however, the attitude and order of the people were correct. It was
just a matter of laying the foundation, not *how* to but *when*.

Ezra 3:7
They gave money also unto the masons, and to the carpenters;
and meat, and drink, and oil, unto them of Zidon, and to them of
Tyre, to bring cedar trees from Lebanon to the sea of Joppa,
according to the grant that they had of Cyrus king of Persia.

The people of God gave:

1. Money – this is the funding of the project. The Spirit of
   Sowing within the House. (The spirit of blessing within the
   ministry)
2. Masons (brick) – ministers dealing with enclosing the house so
   that it is not exposed. This ministry represents the intercessors.
   (This is a prayer ministry)

3. Carpenters – the builders and framers of the ministry (this ministry represents the Teaching ministry within the house)
4. Meat – (the will of God) John 4:34 *"My meat is to do the will of him that sent me, and to finish his work."* The will of God has first priority. (this represents the attitude within the ministry)
5. Drink – (the new wine) those who have been revived. Mt. 9:17 the Spirit of Revival. (this represents the Spirit within the ministry)
6. Oil – unity and anointing Psalms 133 and Psalms 23. The Spirit of unity within the House. (this represents the anointing that is upon the ministry)

The Church gave however; they were giving according to what they heard. They gave according to the Word. The prophetic Word came forth and it stated that the Lord wanted His house built. They acted upon what they believed (faith).

Ezra 3:8
Now in the second year of their coming unto the house of God at Jerusalem, in the second month, began Zerubbabel the son of Shealtiel, and Jeshua the son of Jozadak, and the remnant of their brethren the priests and the Levites, and all they that were come out of the captivity unto Jerusalem; and appointed the Levites, from twenty years old and upward, to set forward the work of the house of the Lord.

The word *second* is connected with the number two. Two is the number for unity. They were actually beginning to function in unity. They came to the very Peace and Certainty of God. In the 2nd month the leaders began to distribute chores (the callings and gifting of those within the house). They were 20 years old and upward. 20 years old is the age of responsibility. They were responsible enough to set forward the work for the House of the Lord. We within ourselves must reach the age of 20 and upward so that we are responsible for the gifting and offices that the Father bestows upon us. The age of 20 and upward represents the spirit of responsibility within the House that is being built. We must be responsible in the first section in order to go on to build the second and the third sections of the House of God.

Ezra 3:10-11
And when the builders laid the foundation of the temple of the LORD, they set the priests in their apparel with trumpets, and the Levites the sons of Asaph with cymbals, to praise the LORD, after the ordinance of David king of Israel.

The foundation was laid, which meant that they could now build the rest of the house. The foundation represents the first floor (it's an individual thing). From an individual standpoint, you have gotten yourself together. You have brought into order everything that was out of order within you. When everything is in order, then we can get a wind (Song of Solomon 4:16).

Ezra 3:12
But many of the priests and Levites and chief of the fathers, who were ancient men, that had seen the first house, when the foundation of this house was laid before their eyes, wept with a loud voice; and many shouted aloud for joy:

Ezra 3:13
So that the people could not discern the noise of the shout of joy from the noise of the weeping of the people: for the people shouted with a loud shout, and the noise was heard afar off.

The word *ancient* is the Hebrew word *zaqen* (zaw-kane'). It means, "to be old; aged man, be (wax) old (man)." It also means "an old man with his chin hanging down." The ancient men wept because they remembered the first house and did not understand the formula of vision and growth. They did not understand Hebrews 6:1 where we are instructed to leave the doctrine (the first or elementary teachings) of Christ and let us go on (bear up) to perfection. The older men with the long chin wept (mourned); however, those who were new and seeing the foundation for the first time "shouted" with joy.

Shouted is the Hebrew word *teruw'ah* (ter-oo-aw'). The root word means "to split the ears;" this word means "an acclamation of joy or a battle-cry;" this word means "an ear splitting acclamation of joy a battle cry." It was a loud shout. It's time to shout it out. Let it be an ear-splitting acclamation of a joyous battle cry, for the Lord has brought us out. He has restored us strengthened us, and has taken us to a higher realm in Him. Yes, it's time to shout loud, shout so that the noise of the

33

weeping is drowned out by the joyous shout of a restored people, shout so that the joyous noise arouses the enemy. Shout, shout, shout, shout, and again I say shout. The noise will be heard which will arouse the enemy.

The Adversaries

> *Ezra 4:1*
> *Now when the adversaries of Judah and Benjamin heard that the children of the captivity builded the temple unto the Lord God of Israel;*

The House of the Lord was being built, Praise God! Whenever there is any type of advancement within the kingdom of God, the enemy gets mad. At this point in the Scripture, the foundation of the House was laid. The house is made of three sections: the foundation, the framing, and the finished product. Because the people went up to Jerusalem (city of Peace), which was in Judah (Praise), the adversaries heard what was going on. The word *adversary* is the Hebrew word *tsar* (tsar). It is from the root word that means "to cramp." This word means "narrow or tight place." The adversary means to cause one to cramp and to place one into a tight place (It's a mental battle). It also means "a stone (as if pressed hard or to a point)." The adversary comes to place you in a cramped, narrow place. Your adversary is a sharp stone that comes to press hard against you. It presses hard because of the advancement that you have made building the first section (the foundation) of the House of God in your life.

The enemy pressed hard against Judah and Benjamin. One of the words for praise is *yadah* (yaw-daw'). It means, "To use the hand as to hold out; as to physically throw a stone or an arrow especially to revere or to worship." The praise of God is the arrow that comes from the believer. We shoot the arrow of praise into the atmosphere that is full of the adversary. The arrow of praise breaks up the atmosphere of the adversary; then our hands are no longer arrows but become the *kaph* (kaf) of praise. What is the *kaph* of praise? It is a word that means, "a hollow hand or palm or dish." Our praises change the position of our hands, which becomes bowls. Once we shoot the praise into the atmosphere of the enemy, the atmosphere is broken up; then the Lord comes down and fills those hands of cups.

The adversary is a stone, and praise is an arrow. Which of the two will overcome the other? As for me I will bless the Lord at all times and His praises (Judah) shall continually be in my mouth (Palms. 34:1). The word *Benjamin* means "the Son of the right hand." Another term for that is "the sons of authority," which is a strong tribe. Benjamin is the Hand of the Lord while Judah is the praises of the Lord. The enemy came against the praise and the authority. How should the adversary of the building project of the Lord be dealt with? Let the strong tribe Benjamin shoot Judah into the adversary. What will this do? It will break up the adversary: "Let God arise, let his enemies be scattered" (Psalms 68:1). It will scatter the adversary into pieces causing that hold to break. Do not let the adversary stop the praises and the authority of God, for if there is no praise, then there can be no peace.

> *Ezra 4:2*
> *Then they came to Zerubbabel, and to the chief of the fathers, and said unto them, Let us build with you: for we seek your God, as ye do; and we do sacrifice unto him since the days of Esarhaddon king of Assur, which brought us up hither.*

The adversaries of the Jews prevented the building of the temple till the reign of Darius. The adversaries heard that the community, which had returned from captivity, was beginning to rebuild the temple, so they came to Zerubbabel and to the chiefs of the people and desired to take part in this work because they also offered to the God of Israel.

These adversaries were the people whom Esarhaddon, king of Assyria, had settled in the neighborhood of Benjamin and Judah. Compare 2 Kings 17:24; the king of Assyria brought men from Cutnah, and from Ava, and from Hamath, and from Sepharvaim, and placed them in the cities of Samaria, and that they took possession of the depopulated kingdom of the ten tribes, and dwelt therein; then these adversaries of Judah and Benjamin are the inhabitants of the former kingdom of Israel, who were called Samaritans after the central-point of their settlement.

> *Ezra 4:3-4*
> *But Zerubbabel, and Jeshua, and the rest of the chief of the fathers of Israel, said unto them, Ye have nothing to do with us to build an house unto our God; but we ourselves together will*

build unto the Lord God of Israel, as king Cyrus the king of
Persia hath commanded us. Then the people of the land weakened
the hands of the people of Judah, and troubled them in building,

Take a stand! The Church is a mighty thing. You the believer are mighty in God (Phil. 4:13) and do not need any help from the enemy. If you allow the enemy in, then you will have to march to the beat of his drum. The Lord gave you and His church the charge to build Him a house. If God spoke it, then it shall be done. No, we don't need any help from the enemy, for we the believers, the local ministry, the full complete body of Christ, will build God a house. For this is the commandment from the Lord which was written and proclaimed by Cyrus the king. God decreed it, and the people of God, the very sons of God, agree that the will of the Lord be done (Matt. 6:10).

Since we have taken a stand, the enemy has come in and weakened the hands of those of Judah (praise). This literally means that the hands that were extended were let or cast down. In football, in order to get to the quarterback it is best to go to the weaker side of the quarterback's protection. This house, once again, is made up of three sections. What are the weaknesses within you the individual, the church, and the body? If there is a weakness within the local ministry, the enemy has a means to get in. If the body of Christ will not take a stand and leaves an opening, the enemy can come in. What is it that the enemy has that will affect the believer? Judah was affected. The Praise was affected, stopped, shutdown, fallen, and the hand was no longer extended; the arrow of praise was no longer shot into the air to create an atmosphere of praise. The territory (Ps. 22:3) was inhabited by the adversary.

Ezra 4:5
And hired counsellors against them, to frustrate their purpose,
all the days of Cyrus king of Persia, even until the reign of
Darius king of Persia.

The adversary hired counsellors. The word *hired* is the Hebrew word *sakar* (saw-kar'). This word takes on the meaning of a prosthesis that is a temporary placement for a missing body part. They had people act on a temporary basis to stop the work of God. They hired temporarily counselors to frustrate the work. The word *frustrate* is the Hebrew word *'aphec* (aw-face') which means "to cause to disappear, cease, be gone (at an end brought to naught), fail." The adversary defeated those who were

36

not of the House of Israel but were a temporary replacement. They acquired people for a temporary purpose. That purpose was totally to stop the House of God from being built. They were hired, assigned temporarily to cause the work to disappear, cease, be clean gone, brought to an end, brought to naught, and most importantly, to fail.

> *Ezra 4:6-7*
> *And in the reign of Ahasuerus, in the beginning of his reign, wrote they unto him an accusation against the inhabitants of Judah and Jerusalem. And in the days of Artaxerxes wrote Bishlam, Mithredath, Tabeel, and the rest of their companions, unto Artaxerxes king of Persia; and the writing of the letter was written in the Syrian tongue, and interpreted in the Syrian tongue.*

Historically speaking as we embark into the 6th and 7th verses of Ezra chapter 4, we are seeing the 4th and 5th kings. At this time Ahasuerus, also known as Xerxes I was on the throne. While he was reigning, there were some accusations that were related to the king. The word *accusation* is the Hebrew word *sitnah* (sit-naw'). It is an opposition (by letter). The word *sitnah* comes from the Hebrew word *satan* (saw-tan') which means, "to attack, accuse, be an adversary, resist." Let us look into Revelation 12:10.

> *Rev. 12:10*
> *And I heard a loud voice saying in heaven, Now is come salvation, and strength, and the kingdom of our God, and the power of his Christ: for the accuser of our brethren is cast down, which accused them before our God day and night.*

The Greek word for *accuser* here is the word *kategoros* (kat-ay'-gor-os), which means "to be against one in the assembly, a complainant at law; satan: accuser." It is made up of two words *kata*, which means "down (in place or time)," and *agora* (ag-or-ah'); which means "the town-square (as a place of public resort); a market or thoroughfare: market (-place), street." *Kategoros* does not only deal with accusations, but those accusations come at a specific time and place, which means to put you on public display! The accuser is satan, the enemy. The word *enemy* is the Hebrew word *'oyeb* (o-yabe') which means "to be an adversary to any one, to persecute Him as an enemy, to hate." The original idea is to be that of breathing, blowing, puffing, and an idea of ten applied to anger and hatred.

The enemy is breathing, blowing, huffing and puffing because of the progress that you, the individual, are making. He is upset because as you become built, the local ministry is also becoming built causing the Complete Body of Christ to become that place that is built upon the Rock, Jesus Christ. The gates of hell cannot, will not prevail against the very Church of the Lord Jesus Christ.

From the Greek word *kategoros* we get the English word *categorize*. This word means "a division used in classification." It also means "a group, kind, or class." The accusation was a letter of opposition, which was an attack from satan, the adversary. This accusation went against those who were the inhabitants of Judah (Praise) and Jerusalem (the Peace of God), and it came at a specific date, time, and place. The accuser comes to categorize the very church of God. It is also important to note when these accusations came. They came when the people got the foundation built. Just as you, the believer, are being built up in God (Jude 20), the accusations come from the enemy at a specific place and time. The place is while you are in Jerusalem (the peace of God); the time is when you finished the foundation and began to shout.

> Ezra 4:7
> *And in the days of Artaxerxes wrote Bishlam, Mithredath, Tabeel, and the rest of their companions, unto Artaxerxes king of Persia; and the writing of the letter was written in the Syrian tongue, and interpreted in the Syrian tongue.*

At this time a new king had come on the scene. The accusation started with Ahasuerus (Xerxes I) and continued with Artaxerxes. This was a long accusation which started in the garden and continued through Job (the oldest book of the Bible); the enemy has been the accuser of the brethren ever since. Three people are named: Bishlam, Mithredath, and Tabeel who were those who wrote letters to the king. These three reveal the unholy trinity mentioned in the book of Revelation: the dragon, the beast, and the false prophet. The three represented in verse 7 reveal the direction of coming attacks. The accusations come to affect three areas. Bishlam's name means "peace" (the enemy comes to attack your peace), your spirit. Mithredath's name means "intellect," and he represents one who searches the law (this spirit comes to show how intelligent it is and attempts to override the Spirit of God) (2 Cor. 10:4-5). This attack comes to attack your soul (mind). The third person is Tabeel, whose name means

"God is good." He represents a false good or a false sense of prosperity. It is a message of prosperity that gives false balances. It teaches "to seek ye first the things" and secondly "if you have time the kingdom of heaven." This spirit comes to attack your body. The accusations come to attack your spirit, soul, and your body. In the second division of the House of God, the enemy comes to attack the spirit of the local ministry (unity within the House), the soul of the local ministry (one mind), and the body (complete church) of the Local ministry.

The letters went against the three-sectioned house: the foundation, the framing, and then the finished product. It attacks three realms: the spirit, the soul, and the body of the believer. If the foundation of the house is hindered, then the rest of the building project will be stalled. The letters were an attack against the peace, intellect, and prosperity, which have taken place in Judah (Praise) in the city of Peace (Jerusalem). The accuser comes to put one on public display (embarrassment), a particular group, kind, or class of people. Those people are they who live in Judah in the city of Jerusalem.

The letter was written in the Syrian tongue, and interpreted in the Syrian tongue. The Syrian tongue is the tongue of the heathen, the tongue of the non-believer. The letter written in Syrian represents the accusations coming from various civic organizations that are antichrist. The Syrian-written letter is one of slander. It is from an unholy trinity who are antichrist and whose minds have not been changed. It is a letter that comes to attack one's spirit, soul, and body. This type of letter represents a false sense of security.

The Syrian tongue is a language of people whose minds have not been changed, and if their minds are not changed they will slander others. Many of you today attempt to communicate your testimony of the good news of God (what He is doing in your life as He builds you) to those who speak the Syrian tongue. They are not happy to see the glory of the Lord upon you, yet you continuously attempt to speak with them. It will not work, for there is a language barrier. They will only speak slander because their minds have not been changed. They will only speak what they know (the Syrian tongue).

What letters of slander have you received? Which tongue has it been written in? The letter is to stop the House of God from being built.

If the enemy has invested actual time in stopping you, the believer, then you must really be important to the purpose of God. The unholy trinity does not want to see the house of God built but the foundation is already laid. God is doing a "New" thing in you, and it shall spring forth. The foundation of God's house (the believer) is being built; allow His perfect work to be done in you.

There were many that jumped on the bandwagon of accusations to stop the building of the House of God. The period of accusations went so long that kings had come and gone. Those who got involved with the attempts to stop the building were people who used their influence with the king so that the Jews could be intimidated.

> *Ezra 4:10*
> *And the rest of the nations whom the great and noble Asnapper brought over, and set in the cities of Samaria, and the rest that are on this side the river, and at such a time.*

Asnapper was referred to as the "great" and "noble." *Great* is the Hebrew word *rab* which means "captain, chief, great, lord, master, stout." The word *noble* means "rare." This king was a rare captain, or chief. The dragon in Revelation 12:3 was a "great red dragon." Asnapper represents the great red dragon, the enemy. He brought over and set in the cities (Churches). He set opposition in the midst of the churches as they were beginning to build the Temple.

> *Gen. 3:14*
> *And the Lord God said unto the serpent, Because thou hast done this, thou art cursed above all cattle, and above every beast of the field; upon thy belly shalt thou go, and dust shalt thou eat all the days of thy life:*

Asnapper represents the accuser. The accuser is the enemy who is the cursed, detestable, evil thing. The accuser desires to curse as he is already cursed. The accuser operates in total doubt. The word *doubt* means "to separate from the truth." The accuser speaks against the Word of God, and not only does he speak against the Word of God but also against the people of God. The accuser comes to totally frustrate or even stop the very vision that has brought you forth thus far in the Peace of God.

Ezra 4:11-16 NIV[2]

(This is a copy of the letter they sent him.) To King Artaxerxes, From your servants, the men of Trans-Euphrates: The king should know that the Jews who came up to us from you have gone to Jerusalem and are rebuilding that rebellious and wicked city. They are restoring the walls and repairing the foundations. Furthermore, the king should know that if this city is built and its walls are restored, no more taxes, tribute or duty will be paid, and the royal revenues will suffer. Now since we are under obligation to the palace and it is not proper for us to see the king dishonored, we are sending this message to inform the king, so that a search may be made in the archives of your predecessors. In these records you will find that this city is a rebellious city, troublesome to kings and provinces, a place of rebellion from ancient times. That is why this city was destroyed. We inform the king that if this city is built and its walls are restored, you will be left with nothing in Trans-Euphrates.

Look at this accusation. See what the enemy thinks of you, the house of God. The work of the Lord is going on within you and within His Church. He is building and restoring the foundations and the walls (Eph. 2:21-22). The walls represent the believers who come together to form the very habitation of God. In this letter I am also noticing selfishness from the king. The king (leader) is a selfish one, and the enemy uses that to his advantage to get the king to bend. Remember, accusations come for a specific place at a specific time. Look at what has happened to this point in your life and the life of the local ministry:

The foundation was laid and you, we the people, shouted.
1. You (individual) shouted because the foundation was laid and finished
2. The (local church) shouted because the foundation of that ministry was laid
3. The (corporate body) shouted because the corporate foundation was laid
4. The walls were set up (the Habitation of the Lord) and the foundations were joined (the spirit of unity Ps. 133: 1-3) as the House of the Lord is being built in this realm.

---

[2] New International Version, (Grand Rapids MI: Zondervan Publishing House 1991)

Because of this good work, the enemy was mad and fabricated a lie. The lie was told of this rebellious city, but this city was the city of Peace that lies within the Praise (Judah) of God. This is a letter of accusation and opposition. It is a taunt from the enemy (accuser); it's an attempt to pummel the church. It was also a letter that dealt with an emotional and selfish king. It declares that if the people progress, their progress would affect the king in the following ways:

1. The king would suffer financially (the money)
2. The King's honor would suffer (the pride)
3. The king's kingdom would suffer (the house would suffer).

Proverbs 29:12
If a ruler hearken to lies, all his servants are wicked.

The mentality of the leader comes into question. How many pastors today have become so full of themselves that they lose compassion for the people? The enemy talked to the king to show the king what he would lose. Many leaders today look to the ministry as a safe haven (means of support), a job. God is kicked out of the house. The people are only a means of support for the personal lives and ministry of the king (leader). Their mentality is "if we get more people, we'll get more money." The church is their only means of income (instead of the Lord). If you (the believer) grow and become built, they become afraid and intimidated that they will lose their money, esteem, and house. So they use force by any means to stop you (or to keep you under them). Another term for stopping you is "hindering" your growth within the Kingdom; you will not be built; you will never become an individual, local ministry, or Corporate House that God is calling for. Remember, "Build Me (God) a House."

Not only can leaders stop (hinder) you as an individual, but they can also stop the local church. They will try to disconnect the members from the umbilical cord that which connects you to your source (Christ), for it is He who feeds and structures you. The accusers and enemies attempt to sever you from Christ. They try to sever you from a place of truth and manna; from a habitation and place of peace, certainty (faith). The accuser comes to sever you from Christ and from you building Him a house. They accuser called this place a "rebellious city." This is not a rebellious city; this is a peaceful city, for the city is called Jerusalem, which is the Shalom of God. This city lies in the province of Judah (the Praises of God).

> *Ezra 4:21-23*
> *Give ye now commandment to cause these men to cease, and that this city be not builded, until another commandment shall be given from me. Take heed now that ye fail not to do this: why should damage grow to the hurt of the kings? Now when the copy of king Artaxerxes' letter was read before Rehum, and Shimshai the scribe, and their companions, they went up in haste to Jerusalem unto the Jews, and made them to cease by force and power.*

The building program was stopped. The building of the individual (the believer) has stopped. The building of the local ministry has stopped; and the expansion of the corporate body or Christ has been halted because of the accuser. The term "made them cease by force and power" is believed to mean that an army was used to stop the building project. In other words, the accusations from the accuser produced an onslaught, an attack from the enemy (Eph. 6:12). Remember, the accusations come from the enemy. He is the father of lies. The lies are birthed within the very belly of the enemy. The accusations are set for a specific place and time. The time to build was in the hearts and minds of the people. They made huge progress. They left Babylon and went up to Jerusalem, which was in Judah. The people became "One Man" and built the foundation. After the foundation was laid, it was time for the second phase. Between the first and the second phase the attack came, and the people of God were ordered and forced to stop.

> *Jer. 29:10*
> *For thus saith the Lord, That after seventy years be accomplished at Babylon I will visit you, and perform my good word toward you, in causing you to return to this place.*

My brothers and sisters in Christ what has stopped you? What word or accusation did you receive that made you stop? What attack did the accuser send? Whatever it was, it came from your adversary, the devil. Jeremiah told us in Jeremiah 29:10 that the Lord would visit us and perform his "good word" towards us, causing us to come back to Jerusalem, the place of peace, which is in Judah (His praises).

43

The commandment and decreeing of the Lord was stopped through the means of accusations from the enemy. It stopped in the 2nd year of Darius the King. It stopped just when you, the individual, were starting to reach out to your brothers and sisters and understand that you are in covenant with them. The work stopped at the time when the local churches were starting to be in covenant with one another regardless of race or denomination. It stopped when the true Body of Christ was beginning to form itself. The amount of time between Ezra 4:24 and Ezra 5:1 is 15 years. The building project stopped for 15 years. Many that are reading this book have stopped building; you have set yourself in the sidelines for 15 years because of what the accusations had set out to do towards you.

Chapter Four

Get Back to Work

Ezra 5:1
Then the prophets, Haggai the prophet, and Zechariah the son of
Iddo, prophesied unto the Jews that were in Judah and Jerusalem
in the name of the God of Israel, even unto them.

The prophet Haggai's name means "festive." The Prophet
Zechariah's name means "God has remembered." The word *remember*
means "to mark (so as to be recognized), to mark for a specific time." God
has marked you for His purpose at a particular time. The festive (praise)
of the Lord is speaking and the Lord who remembers (who has marked
you for a specific time) is speaking to cause the People to get back to
where and what God has decreed for them to do. God raised up the
prophets (we need a Word from the Lord) Haggai and Zechariah to stir up
the spirits of the believers that they might continue the rebuilding of the
Temple.

Ezekiel prophesied, "O ye dry bones, hear the word of the Lord."
There must be a word from the Lord. The enemy was breathing, blowing
fires of accusations against God's people. However, God is breathing and
blowing a Word into His people in this day and time. The fire of God has
intensified upon the altar and also upon the lips of His prophets. The word
of the Lord for this hour is a hot one, coming from the very heart and lips
of God, Hallelujah! This Word from the Lord is a "Good Word" that is
going to be performed in the midst of His people. This word will cause
those who have stopped building to return to the Jerusalem of God that is
in Judah. Your praise has stopped, and because the praise has stopped,

there is not peace. But your praise is getting ready to start again, and from the praise comes the very peace of God. The word of the Lord is here.

To get a clear understanding as to what was happening at this stage of the building project, we will go over to the book of Haggai. We can pick up the story there.

> *Haggai 1:1-2*
> *In the second year of Darius the king, in the sixth month, in the first day of the month, came the word of the Lord by Haggai the prophet unto Zerubbabel the son of Shealtiel, governor of Judah, and to Joshua the son of Josedech, the high priest, saying, Thus speaketh the Lord of hosts, saying, This people say, The time is not come, the time that the Lord's house should be built.*

The people have become so settled for what the enemy has brought to them that when the prophets declared the Word of the Lord, they (the people) said, IT'S NOT TIME YET. This is a cry and confession of submission and defeat. How many of the believers are saying this very thing today? Many have gifts and callings upon your life. God is calling for you, yet you tell God "It's not time yet." Why are the people of God confessing this? They confess this because of fear. The house of God today is not being built because many are afraid of what it will cost them. The wounds of the past are continuing to hurt in the heart, and so the mentality of many of the called and chosen is that I don't want to be hurt anymore, so I'll just sit on the sidelines and do nothing. The accusations from the enemy have put a hold on the believer for over 15 years. Yes, you have been doing nothing for over 15 years. The "it is not time yet" mentality is a strong act of doubt against faith when the work of the kingdom is involved.

That time will never come as long as you continue to be afraid. You built the foundation, but that is as far as you have gotten. The word of the Lord has come to you this day, my brother and my sister, to tell you that it's time to go up to Jerusalem and finish what God has started in you [*Being confident of this very thing, that he which hath begun a good work in you will perform it until the day of Jesus Christ* (Phil. 1:6).]

> *Hag. 1:4*
> *Is it time for you, O ye, to dwell in your ceiled houses, and this house lie waste?*

Sad to say that many dwell today in their ceiled houses, and those ceiled houses have become "sealed" houses. The sealed house is one that is shut off and away from everyone. Your company has become a four-walled box, a place that you have settled in. This process has caused the real you, the House of God, to lie waste! But the Word of the Lord is declared and decreed unto you this day. Consider your ways. In other words, put your heart back where it belongs. Your heart belongs in the building project of the Lord.

Hag. 1:8
Go up to the mountain, and bring wood, and build the house; and I will take pleasure in it, and I will be glorified, saith the Lord.

How do we, the church, get back into the plan of God? How can you get back into working order? How do we start work for its time to work? The prophet says, "Go up to the mountain." This command refers to sacrifice and true worship. "Bring wood" speaks of sacrifice the 10th day of the 7th month (the Day of Atonement or the day or repentance). This sacrifice represents a time of forgiveness and repentance. "Build the house" simply means to get back to the original decreed Vision of God which is to take place in 3 realms. Once this process is done, God will take pleasure (this word refers to one who satisfies a debt) in the house (the three sectioned house), and He will be glorified (this is a place huge enough and strong enough to handle His glory, which is His actual weight).

Hag. 1: 9-11
Ye looked for much, and, lo, it came to little; and when ye brought it home, I did blow upon it. Why? saith the Lord of hosts. Because of mine house that is waste, and ye run every man unto his own house. Therefore the heaven over you is stayed from dew, and the earth is stayed from her fruit. And I called for a drought upon the land, and upon the mountains, and upon the corn, and upon the new wine, and upon the oil, and upon that which the ground bringeth forth, and upon men, and upon cattle, and upon all the labour of the hands.

There has been a hold-up in our personal lives. The reason is because God's house does lie in wait. God is saying that nothing will be released to the believer until we put His house, His work first. We are to seek ye first His kingdom. Notice the areas that are affected because of our stagnation and procrastination:

1. God blew on what you brought home because it was not of Him, and because His house is not built nothing that you put your hands to will be built (this happens in 3 realms)
2. Heaven over you is stayed from dew (the will of God will not be released into something that is unfinished or not ready)
3. The earth is stayed from dew (no growth into the kingdom)
4. God called for a drought upon your land (no prosperity)
5. God called for a drought upon the mountains (no expansion of worship and praise)
6. God called for a drought upon the corn (no vision)
7. God called for a drought upon the new wine (no fresh revelation)
8. God called for a drought upon our oil (no anointing)
9. God called for a drought upon that which the ground brings forth (no increase)
10. God called for a drought upon men (no fellowship, no priesthood within the homes).
11. God called for a drought upon the cattle (no blessing or provision)
12. God called for a drought upon the labour of the hands (no jobs to support the kingdom work).

God held back the rain (no moisture) 2 Chron. 6:46-7:14; Hanna's (who represents the believer) womb is shut because the Lord shut up her womb (no birthing of vision) 1 Sam. 1:5; there is no rain or birthing of vision because we, the church, after building the foundation have stopped building the rest of the House. We have become preoccupied and also have come to a point where we now remain in our ceiled (sealed) house, which is a place of our security and hiding. However, the Word of the Lord is here and He is saying to leave that place.

After the prophet brought the Word of the Lord to the people, the desire began to come back. The only way God will resurrect His vision within His people is through the means of an anointed, prophetic Word.

48

Hag. 1:12

Then Zerubbabel the son of Shealtiel, and Joshua the son of Josedech, the high priest, with all the remnant of the people, obeyed the voice of the Lord their God, and the words of Haggai the prophet, as the Lord their God had sent him, and the people did fear before the Lord.

The Word of the Lord came and the people obeyed or heard intelligently. They become not only hearers but also doers of His Word.

Ezra 5:1-3

Then the prophets, Haggai the prophet, and Zechariah the son of Iddo, prophesied unto the Jews that were in Judah and Jerusalem in the name of the God of Israel, even unto them. Then rose up Zerubbabel the son of Shealtiel, and Jeshua the son of Jozadak, and began to build the house of God which is at Jerusalem: and with them were the prophets of God helping them. At the same time came to them Tatnai, governor on this side the river, and Shetharboznai, and their companions, and said thus unto them, Who hath commanded you to build this house, and to make up this wall?

Let us return to Ezra 5:1-3. After the message of Haggai went forth, it was met by great opposition. Men called Tatanai and Shetharboznai immediately tested what the prophets spoke. Tatanai and Shetharboznai were opposed to the resuming of the building project. The name Tatanai means "my gifts." He was the governor of one side of the river. He represents the world and the flesh. The Shetharboznai means "the enforcer or authority." Tatanai was the governor of the flesh or gifts (antichrists) while Shetharboznai was the enforcer of those gifts. Those gifts are in Eph. 6:11, principalities, powers, rulers of the darkness of this world, and spiritual wickedness in high places. Shetharboznai is the enforcer of these wicked gifts. The enemy and his enforcers challenged the Prophetic Word of the Lord. Notice what they said: "Who has commanded you to build this house and to make up this wall? In other words, who has given you the right to continue the vision of God and to make up this habitation of the Lord? The enemy hates the idea of the people of God progressing. The enemy is total doubt, confusion, and discord amongst the brethren. He hates the decreed word.

49

Ezra 6:1-2
Then Darius the king made a decree, and search was made in the house of the rolls, where the treasures were laid up in Babylon. And there was found at Achmetha, in the palace that is in the province of the Medes, a roll, and therein was a record thus written:

The enemy enforcers challenged the very word of God that has been prophesied over your life, local church, and Body of Christ. However they searched the record; they searched the Word and realized that the right for the Jews to build was already in force. It was given way back when Cyrus was living. A few things to keep in mind about what the Lord God is revealing in this passage:
God knew:
1. There would be opposition
2. There would be an accuser that would present a letter of slander
3. There would be a king that would write a decree demanding that you stop.

But it was too late; the Word of the Lord had already been decreed over your life before you were born. What the believer must do is agree and walk in what has been decreed. What did God decree over your life? God decreed:

1. That you should go up to Jerusalem (the city of Peace), that you should have peace
2. That you should go to Judah (Praises), that you should live in the Praise of God
3. That His house shall be built (you will become the House of God)
4. That His house shall be built (we shall build God a House (a local ministry)
5. That His House shall be built (we shall become the corporate House of God, the body of Christ)

Heb. 11:3
Through faith we understand that the worlds were framed by the word of God, so that things which are seen were not made of things which do appear.

The decreed word of the Lord is what is standing under you. God, according to Hebrews 11:3, has framed the ages by the Word and upholds (stands under or supports) all things by His power. He is standing under that which He has decreed over your life. When did He speak this? According to Ephesians 1:4, while we were chosen in Him. When was that? Before the foundation or conception of the world.

Ezra 6:6
Now therefore, Tatnai, governor beyond the river, Shetharboznai, and your companions the Apharsachites, which are beyond the river, be ye far from thence:

After the Word of the Lord was found, preached, and established within the people, the King sent word to Tatnai to be ye far from thence; in other words "move out of the way."

Ezra 6:14
And the elders of the Jews builded, and they prospered through the prophesying of Haggai the prophet and Zechariah the son of Iddo. And they builded, and finished it, according to the commandment of the God of Israel, and according to the commandment of Cyrus, and Darius, and Artaxerxes king of Persia.

During the time of my teaching this series called "Build Me a House," which is a series of teachings from the book of Ezra, we were in Bible study one Thursday evening, and the Holy Spirit began to speak to our ministry. That Thursday night the hearts of the people became so uplifted because of what the Holy Spirit was revealing from the teaching that a thunderous praise broke forth in the midst of that Thursday evening Bible study, and then the Holy Spirit began to minister. As the Spirit ministered, he opened my naked eyes, and I began to see in a vision various things within the ministry. He told me to share it with the church, and so I did as I was commanded and would now also like to share part of that vision with you, the reader.

In the vision, the Lord revealed to me what He sees within His church, and also it was revealed what God desires to do through His people. In that vision I saw what Ezekiel saw, which was a mountain of bones. In that vision were also other bones that were scattered throughout a field. The Lord spoke and said that the mountains of bones and the scattered bones represent two dilemmas. The first dilemma is seen with the mountain of bones. That vision represents many who have stopped. The second dilemma is noticed in the scattered bones. That vision represents those who have been wounded and have lost strength to continue. They have stopped functioning, the house has ceased from being built, and they have remained in nothing but a huge mountain and a scattered bone in a huge field sealed off from walking in their complete destiny. The Lord continued to share with me how He desired to relieve them of that for they must get back to building God a House.

In the beginning of this book I said that there is one agenda and that is that His House be built. Then the Lord told us on that night to build, and then He will use us to cause others to go up to Jerusalem, which is in Judah, to build. The last thing that God told us on that beautiful and prophetic night was that He desires to be built within His people.

The commandment of the Lord is here. Go back up and build. Get back to work. We have put His agenda aside for 15 years, and now it is time. The enemy keeps telling you that it is not time yet and that those whom you know will not respect you for the gifting and work that is in you to do. But God has already anointed you and me to do what He has called us to do. Samuel the prophet has already visited you at the house of Jesse and poured the oil upon your head. It's time for Hannah to have her baby because now her womb (place that houses promise) is opened by the Lord. It is about to rain, so it is time.

Ezra 6:15
And this house was finished on the third day of the month Adar, which was in the sixth year of the reign of Darius the king.

After Haggai preached, it took 23 days to finish the House of the Lord. It only took 23 days. This means the temple was almost finished when they stopped 15 years ago. Many have come so far and have given up. But the Word of the Lord comes to you now to tell you to "get back to work."

Chapter Five

The Finished House

Ezra 6:15
And this house was finished on the third day of the month Adar,
which was in the sixth year of the reign of Darius the king. And
the children of Israel, the priests, and the Levites, and the rest of
the children of the captivity, kept the dedication of this house of
God with joy,

After finally getting to Jerusalem, Judah, to build God a house, the
house was finished in the month of Adar. Adar is the 12th month of the
Hebrew calendar, and 12 is the number for government and order. Things
were in order, so the house was able to be finished. The children of Israel
also kept the dedication of this house of God with joy. The word
dedication is the Hebrew word *Chanukah* (Hanukkah). It is the biblical
holiday that celebrates the "Feast of Lights" or "Feast of Dedication."
This day is the celebration of Lights (candle lights). In the tabernacle the
seven-branded candlestick is what gives light to the dark sanctuary. That
light represented the revelation of Jesus Christ. It is the lighting of the
eternal flame in your spirit, the illumination of His life, which is the light
of men. This day of dedication is the celebration of the revelation of Jesus
Christ. The house of God must have this light within its ministry; if there
is no revelation of Jesus, then there is no Jesus.

Ezra 6:17
And offered at the dedication of this house of God an hundred
bullocks, two hundred rams, four hundred lambs; and for a sin
offering for all Israel, twelve he goats, according to the number of
the tribes of Israel.

a. 100 Bullocks - Full and complete sacrifice and surrender
b. 200 Rams – Full witness of dedication
c. 400 Lambs – Full atonement for creation
d. 12 He Goats – For a sin offering for all Israel (12 tribes).

Ezra 6:19
And the children of the captivity kept the passover upon the fourteenth day of the first month.

The Hebrew word for Passover is *pecach*. The root word means "to hop, skip over to hesitate;" it also literally means "to limp, to dance." The first of the three annual festivals was the Passover. It commemorated Israel's deliverance. The Passover took place on the fourteenth day (at evening) of the first month (Lev. 23:5). The Passover reveals one jumping over the enemy, which means we have jumped over all obstacles that have attempted to hinder the House of God from being built within me (three realms). It is the celebration of our deliverance. The church kept (accomplished) the celebration of its deliverance. The Church celebrated the jumping over or crossing over the roadblocks. It was on the 14th day (the number for deliverance).

Ezra 6:20-22
For the priests and the Levites were purified together, all of them were pure, and killed the passover for all the children of the captivity, and for their brethren the priests, and for themselves.

The Body of Christ (the finished House) killed the Lamb and ate the Lamb. It reveals how that when the Israelites left Egypt, they ate a Lamb and that Lamb was able to sustain them as they were going through their time of Deliverance. The children that once lived in Babylon, the brethren, and the ministers all ate the Lamb. The House of God was a joyous House. Their hearts were joyful because the house was finished (a corporate Man); the heart of the king of Assyria was turned unto them to strengthen their hands to continue to work on the House of God. The Priest and the Levites (ministers) were purified together. Today, we, the believers, are purified together. We have become a holy and separated people. We became the pure Body of Christ, One Corporate (Man). The church is now purified from the filthiness of the heathen in the land. We do not bring the world into the Church, but bring the Church into the

54

World. We do not develop the mind of the world but the mind of Christ. We also continually eat the unleavened bread (His Word) for seven days (consecration).

Ezra 7:1
Now after these things, in the reign of Artaxerxes king of Persia,
Ezra the son of Seraiah, the son of Azariah, the son of Hilkiah,

Between chapters 6 and 7, 80 years have transpired. In chapter 7 we are introduced to Ezra. Ezra was a ready scribe in the Law of Moses. What is a ready scribe? It is one who is skillful in writing, communicating the history and Word of the Lord. Actually the term "ready scribe" means that he was one who flowed easily. Ezra's calling was to write and instruct the Law of Moses (The Word). Ezra was one who flowed easily into his destiny. Because of His calling and his functioning in that call, the Lord blessed Ezra with favor of king Artaxerxes (Proverbs 3:1-6).

In Ezra chapter 7 verses 7-9 we meet another group of people coming out of Babylon (place of an overflowing confusion) to Jerusalem (the place of peace). Prophetically this time reveals the Feast of Tabernacles, which is a time of world Harvest. These groups of people represent the influx of souls that will take place after the house of God is built. First there had to be a foundation (the individual). After the foundation is laid, then it is time for the local ministry to be built (the framing of the house). The local ministry must be built with a group of people who have a deep foundation because they are the pillars. After the pillars are built, then it is time for the second group or the second stage.

The second stage is the time of harvest. It is a reaping time, a time of receiving for all that was planted into the kingdom. This second group will have to travel the same way and will take the same amount of time to become a built foundation as it did with the first group. It took the first group four months. The second group will have to travel the same route; however there will be many coaches from the set house that will help them to travel. Ezra led these people to Jerusalem because he was anointed to do it, for "the good hand of the Lord" was upon him. The good hand is the hand of favour (Prov. 3:1-6).

As previously mentioned Ezra flowed easy in his destiny. He wrote prophetically. That calling and functioning in the prophetic causes the scribe to walk in the favor (Proverbs 3:1-6) of God and man. What are scribes? They are those who will seek the Lord, do the Law, and teach the Law. Scribes are Prophets who serve as the fingers of the Holy Spirit. Scribes have the spirit of the Eagle (Deut. 32:11; Job 39:27-30). They write as the Holy Spirit speaks, and those words are inscribed on the walls of the Hearts of the people (Heb. 8:10). Their calling calls for a sacrifice and anointing right ear, the right hand, and the great right toe (Ex. 29:20). The right ear is sacrificed so that that ear can hear the spirit of the Lord. The right thumb is sacrificed so that it can be used to write of the Words of the Lord. The great right toe is sacrificed to walk in the direction of the Lord. This all speaks of sacrificing (being placed upon the altar), and the scribe must understand that it will take a sacrificing of oneself in order to write prophetically in this day and time. Ezra here represents the gifting of the Lord being added to the ministry when the structure is built.

We must become all three: a foundation, a local ministry and then the corporate body. After the temple was built, it became FULL of the glory of the Lord. The temple of the Lord becomes His pleasure since He is glorified in it. When the church becomes finished, then it becomes full. Then the Lord begins to work out of that place; it becomes impregnated with vision. The church becomes full of the Holy Ghost.

> *Matt. 1:20*
> *But while he thought on these things, behold, the angel of the Lord appeared unto him in a dream, saying, Joseph, thou son of David, fear not to take unto thee Mary thy wife: for that which is conceived in her is of the Holy Ghost.*

The Holy Ghost wants to impregnate Mary (the Church). After the local ministry is built, it must get impregnated. It must be impregnated with Jesus, the Christ child, and it can only happen when we walk in our destiny. Ezra must write as he listens to the Words of the Holy Spirit; then those words must be imparted into the believer. When those words are imparted into the believer, the believer then looks for the Holy Spirit to drop the Seed into that spirit, and then in nine months that which is conceived shall come forth. Once we begin to walk in what we have been taught, we will be walking in our destiny.

To walk in destiny means to walk in what God has called you to and not to stop. Your local ministry cannot stop. To stop means that you have failed, and every failure is nothing more than a broken focus. To stop simply means you have lost focus; in other words, you have allowed the enemy to distract you. However, Ezra is here writing you telling you that you must get the vision of God back into focus, for Mary the virgin is here, and it is time for her to:

1. Get full of the Holy Ghost
2. Become the full (Whole) House (Ezek. 37:14)
3. Get pregnant
4. Bring forth a Son
5. Name that son Jesus; Live up to that name, which means salvation (to a lost world), and deliverance (to a lost world)
6. Teach in that Name (Jesus).

Out of Mary will come not a divided family but a Corporate Son made after the Pattern Son. Those who make up that Corporate Son are:

1. A people for his name (Acts 15:14)
2. A people of His nature
3. A people of all that He is
4. A people of all He has
5. A people of all that He does
6. A people who believe in Sacrificing for the corporate body
7. A people who walk in the Spirit of Restoration
8. A people who ate and are still eating the Lamb at the time of Passover (the remembrance of our deliverance; our testimony)
9. A people who have the spirit of Hanukah (the celebration of Lights which is the Revelation of Jesus Christ)
10. A people who live in Jerusalem, Judah (the peace within the praise)
11. A people of the tribe of Benjamin (sons of the right hand or authority)
12. A people of three dimensions (a laid foundation, structured framing, and the finished thing)
13. A people of the 7th hour.

Haggai 1:8
Go up to the mountain, and bring wood, and build the house; and I will take pleasure in it, and I will be glorified, saith the Lord.

The Word *glorified* is the Hebrew word *kabad* (kaw-bad'). It means "to be heavy or weight." The house must be big and strong and ordered enough to be able to handle the glory or the weight of the Lord. He is going to be pleased with His house, for the house will carry the burden (weight) or glory of the Lord within and in so doing that He will be glorified. Always remember that the earth is the Lord's and not the devil's. It always has been and will always be the Lord's. (Psalms 24:1).

It is time for us to begin to walk in our destiny. You are a finished thing, and His local ministry is a finished thing. Now it is time for the ordered local church to become full of the Holy Ghost so that the body of Christ can be formed. Every thought of failure is a message from the accuser. He has given each and everyone of us the gifting that is needed to build His house. Ezra is now ready to come forth and bring more people up to Jerusalem regardless of how long it takes to travel to that place. It is time for the three-sectioned house to become pregnant, to become full of the Holy Ghost, to become full of scribes and write prophetically and fulfill the very vision of God. We are His Windows through which He functions. It is time to be promoted. *"And I sought for a man among them, that should make up the hedge, and stand in the gap before me for the land, that I should not destroy it: but I found none"* (Ezek. 22:30). However, the man is found, and it is a corporate man (the corporate body of Christ), the one-man in which the people became in Ezra 3:1. It is "A Time to Work" as never before. It is time for Ezra, the Ready Scribe, to come forth and lead the harvest in.

> *Ezra 8:1*
> *These are now the chief of their fathers, and this is the genealogy of them that went up with me from Babylon, in the reign of Artaxerxes the king.*

> *Ezra 8:15*
> *And I gathered them together to the river that runneth to Ahava; and there abode we in tents three days: and I viewed the people, and the priests, and found there none of the sons of Levi.*

Ezra, the ready scribe, got the people "ready" to go up to Jerusalem. It will take someone who is "ready" in order to get the people ready. He then gathered the people together at the river that runs to Ahava. He gathered them at the river. The river represents a flow. People can move only when they have a flow to move. He was ready to

58

go but realized that even though this is the second group making this trip, there still had to be order. The Levites were missing. The ones who were in charge of worship were missing. They had no praise leaders. Remember that Jerusalem is in Judah. It will take praise in order to have the peace, so the Levites are needed. Don't ever get to a point where you think that thanksgiving, praise, and worship are not necessary for the House of God. That is the element that builds the house of God because the praise is the very habitation of God in the midst of His people. I love what Ezra did; he did not make a move until he got the Levites, and he ended up with 37.

They stayed at the River of Ahava for three days (Hosea 6:1-3). This time represents the death, burial, and resurrection, the three levels that all believers, ministries, and the corporate body must go through and never forget. His death, His burial, and His resurrection are what has allowed His corporate body to have the liberty that we now have in order to produce God on planet Earth. Ezra called for a fast. He called for a day when the people would afflict themselves. This day represents a time of the people crying out to God asking for His direction and protection for our families, children, and for our prosperity within the Land which He has promised.

> *Ezra 8:22*
> *For I was ashamed to require of the king a band of soldiers and horsemen to help us against the enemy in the way: because we had spoken unto the king, saying, The hand of our God is upon all them for good that seek him; but his power and his wrath is against all them that forsake him.*

This verse is the most profound verse in the entire book of Ezra. Please understand what he is saying. Ezra says that he called a fast because he was too embarrassed to ask the king to grant them a band of soldiers and horsemen to help them against the enemy on their way. If we are going to preach the Gospel, then we must live that same Gospel. So they sought the Lord and relied on His presence, and the Lord was entreated of them. Because they sought the Lord, He granted them deliverance from all of their enemies that were in the way of them getting to Jerusalem.

This second group going up to Jerusalem being led by Ezra the Scribe represents breakthrough and a breaking forth of a world harvest.

The message had to be written and declared by the Scribe. The journey was a hard one, and the people had to set a time of fasting so that the hearts could become turned to the Lord. Ezra did not move towards Jerusalem until they fasted first. After the fast, they moved out to head towards Jerusalem. Who is this group? They were sons of this one and sons of that one. This harvest represents the believer's children. These groups are those who you have prayed for and sought the Lord for. These represent our loved ones, ones that we have not given up on but have kept them on the altar. Society has called them Generation X, but God calls them His. Yes, I, the scribe of the Lord, being led by the Holy Spirit to write this Word unto you, do prophesy that our Children will come up to Jerusalem and worship the Lord.

> Ezra 8:33-34
> *Now on the fourth day was the silver and the gold and the vessels weighed in the house of our God by the hand of Meremoth the son of Uriah the priest; and with him was Eleazar the son of Phinehas; and with them was Jozabad the son of Jeshua, and Noadiah the son of Binnui, Levites; By number and by weight of every one: and all the weight was written at that time.*

Notice also that this group of people did not come empty handed but brought with them gold, silver, lambs, and many other things. Those things that they brought and will bring represent the gifts that they will offer unto the Lord. Their gifts will be unique gifts. They will be odd to the natural eye but powerful in the sight of God. It will be those gifts that they will use to offer unto the Lord and bring in more harvest for the Lord. As they allow God to use them in their gifting, then "*Herein is my Father glorified*" (John 15:8).

The gold and silver also represent finances. When they started towards Jerusalem, Ezra required an accounting system for the gold and silver. There was 24 tons of silver, approximately 4 tons of silver and gold vessels, and approximately 18 pounds of gold. They fasted before they moved the gold and silver. In other words, they had to pray for protection of the finances. It was important that they be good stewards of the money because money that people give to the House of the Lord is their seed being planted into good ground. If the people intend on receiving a good harvest, then there must be proper planting or managing of that money. There is an important lesson to be learned here from Ezra.

What he did was initiate a strict accounting system, and those over that system were to give an account of that which they oversaw.

It will take finances to build God a house. However the people must be in tune enough to be able to distribute those finances properly. There must be a strict accounting system so that everything that goes into building God a house is accountable and those overseeing that accounting will show their accountability.

Chapter Six

The Falling Away and the Remedy

Ezra 9:1-4
Now when these things were done, the princes came to me,
saying, The people of Israel, and the priests, and the Levites, have
not separated themselves from the people of the lands, doing
according to their abominations, even of the Canaanites, the
Hittites, the Perizzites, the Jebusites, the Ammonites, the
Moabites, the Egyptians, and the Amorites. For they have taken
of their daughters for themselves, and for their sons: so that the
holy seed have mingled themselves with the people of those lands:
yea, the hand of the princes and rulers hath been chief in this
trespass. And when I heard this thing, I rent my garment and
my mantle, and plucked off the hair of my head and of my beard,
and sat down astonied. Then were assembled unto me every one
that trembled at the words of the God of Israel, because of the
transgression of those that had been carried away; and I sat
astonied until the evening sacrifice.

The corporate body cannot ever forget how the Lord has brought us from Babylon and allowed us to come into Jerusalem, Judah. We must never allow ourselves to get to a point where we don't need the Lord. The Lord's house is His house and the only one who can live there is He. If Jezebel gets in, she can kill everything that has been established. If this happens, it will take an intercession from a Scribe (prophet who is the Hands of the Holy Spirit). That intercession will bring the people to weeping sore before the Lord.

Exodus 23:31-33
And I will set thy bounds from the Red sea even unto the sea of
the Philistines, and from the desert unto the river: for I will
deliver the inhabitants of the land into your hand; and thou shalt
drive them out before thee. Thou shalt make no covenant with
them, nor with their gods. They shall not dwell in thy land, lest
they make thee sin against me: for if thou serve their gods, it will
surely be a snare unto thee.

When Ezra returned he received news of the failures and sin of the
people. In Exodus the Law had already been given. The Lord said

1. He would deliver the inhabitants of the land into their
   (Israelites) hands
2. The Israelites should drive the inhabitants out
3. Do not make any covenant with them or their gods.
4. They shall not dwell in their land because they (the
   inhabitants) will cause the believers to sin against God,
   and if the Israelites serve the inhabitants' god it will be
   to the Israelites a snare.

The Israelites did not get the inhabitants out, and the Israelites
made covenant with those inhabitants. They dwelled in the land
(Promised Land) of the Israelites, and the Israelites mingled and then
eventually married them. From those marriages came seed or children.
This happened because though the Israelites were going to build God a
House, they did not drive the enemy out.

The enemy must be driven out of the land of the believers. The
very thing that the Law spoke against became the way of practice for the
Israelites (Church). They mingled so long until they became just like the
world. Not only did they marry out of the faith, but they also followed
after the abominations of the inhabitants; this happened because they did
not drive the enemy out as they were supposed to.

God is speaking to us in this teaching. The Lord is saying, "Build
Me a House." We must be careful how and where we build in the three
realms. The enemy must be driven out. If the enemy is not driven out,
then the enemy will take place and begin to lead.

Rev. 2:20
Notwithstanding I have a few things against thee, because thou
sufferest that woman Jezebel, which calleth herself a prophetess,
to teach and to seduce my servants to commit fornication, and to
eat things sacrificed unto idols.

I want to talk about a person named Jezebel. Jezebel was the wife of King Ahab of Israel (874-853 B.C.). She was responsible for bringing the worship of Baal from Sidon, where her father Ethbaal was king, into Jerusalem. She was anti-god and hated anything to do with the Almighty God, so she attempted to destroy all God's prophets. She eventually was destroyed; however, we read of the name Jezebel again in Revelation 2:20. In the book of 1st Kings Jezebel is a person; however, in the book of Revelation she is seen as a spirit. In essence, she is a teaching spirit that is anti-God and anti-truth. She (Jezebel) is a total lie; she is a separator of truth; she is error, and she is a unity, anointing, and unicity killer. Jezebel is a spiritual teaching, whoring spirit who thrives on the practice of divorce and separation within the kingdom of God.

In my book entitled *A Time to Work* I deal with the subject "unity." Please understand that the church in the book of Ezra was in unity, and they made progress; however, they allowed the enemy to fool them and became separated from the Law by disobeying that Law. How did they disobey? They disobeyed by mingling and marrying non-believers (those who lack faith, revelational insight, and the Holy Spirit to guide them).

The spirit of Jezebel is a unity or union breaker that thrives off of the spirit of divorce. It is this same roaming spirit that hates unity. What is unity? It is the singleness of mind to pursue God's purpose. That singleness of mind must live in an environment where it can thrive and grow. Unity pursues God's purpose, but it must be in an atmosphere where it is functioning in order for unity to be productive. Unity produces life, while divorce, which is of the spirit of Jezebel, produces death. The Israelites in Ezra became separated from the Law of God; they became divorced from the truth through disobedience. A death such as this can happen in a ministry. It is important that we do not absolutely miss the leadership of God or the voice of the Holy Ghost. If the spirit of Jezebel creeps in, it will attempt to release a spiritual whoring, teaching spirit within the people.

Rev. 6:8
And I looked, and behold a pale horse: and his name that sat on him was Death, and Hell followed with him. And power was given unto them over the fourth part of the earth, to kill with sword, and with hunger, and with death, and with the beasts of the earth.

In this passage let's see through the eyes of the Holy Ghost in order to receive the revelation. Death represents the teaching spirit of Jezebel being in full force. Hell following besides death means that the thing death killed is swallowed up in hell so that it is annihilated. What is the thing that death desires to kill? Death desires to kill unity, and hell wants to swallow it up. Death's primary function within the body of Christ is not only to stop the flow of unity but also to stop the House of God from being built. Death hates unity, and if unity is annihilated, then there will be no strength, no life, and no built house.

The Israelites in the book of Ezra became separated from the Word and began to listen to the whoring spirit which told them in essence to disobey the Law of God. They married non-believers, and they separated from unity. When they separated from unity they separated from:

1. The Law
2. The Spirit of Unity
3. The Vision of the House
4. The victory that caused them to triumph
5. Their relationship with God
6. Their Godly relationship with each other (Heb. 13:1) "Let brotherly love continue."
7. Their Godly seed and followed after un-godly seed (Ex. 34:16).

Anything that takes the place of God in your heart becomes your god. It becomes your Jezebel. Lets refer to Revelation 2:20 again. The Lord said he had problems with that Church because they allowed that spiritual whoring spirit to teach. She taught under the title of prophetess, but she was nothing more than a whore. The Greek word for *teach* is *didasko* (did-as'-ko), which means "to cause to know or to impart knowledge." Now the Israelites did not drive out the enemy, so the enemy ended up imparting knowledge to those people. That false doctrinal teacher Jezebel seduced the Church, meaning she was able to cause them to roam and wander. They wandered out of the will of God. She caused them to commit fornication and to eat things sacrificed unto gods, meaning the spirit of Jezebel can cause the people no longer to have communion; there will be no celebration of the Lord's Supper (1 Cor. 11:26).

So what will happen if Jezebel were allowed to teach? She will cause others to wander away from the truth, and she will teach the people to act the harlot, or, in other words, she will teach the people to act like her. Jezebel is no longer the woman who brought baal worship into Israel. No, she has transformed herself into a system. She is no longer killing prophets, but now the system Jezebel is killing generations. She is killing unity and causing men to make un-godly babies. The leaders in the time of this prophecy were allowing this system to rule, dominate, and teach, and that system impregnated the people causing the people to have children. This system can grow throughout generations and become the rule of operation in a local church.

This process can happen within the local church if we leave or become severed from the truth. The spirit of Jezebel will sneak in and begin to teach. The spirit of Jezebel is a spirit of ungodly, unordained teaching within the church. Teaching impregnates whoever or wherever it is allowed to land, and if received in you can impregnate you and cause you to produce whatever un-truth you are impregnated by. What type of Theology are you receiving? Is it one that is allowed by blind leadership that will come forth and influence the people? The teaching received becomes the teaching one eats or is nourished by. Anything that is taught within the local churches outside of the Word of God is a type of pornography. What is pornography? Basically, pornography is a deception. It is a deception that causes one to fall for non-truth. In Ezra they left the law and went a whoring and produced the very seed that God told them not to have. In Revelation 2:23 Jezebel had children, meaning the spirit of Jezebel was able to reproduce her fruit or seed.

Nahum 3:1-4
Woe to the bloody city! it is all full of lies and robbery; the prey departeth not; The noise of a whip, and the noise of the rattling

of the wheels, and of the prancing horses, and of the jumping chariots. The horseman lifteth up both the bright sword and the glittering spear: and there is a multitude of slain, and a great number of carcases; and there is none end of their corpses; they stumble upon their corpses: Because of the multitude of the whoredoms of the wellfavoured harlot, the mistress of witchcrafts, that selleth nations through her whoredoms, and families through her witchcrafts.

Nahum 3:1-4 speaks of a city (Nineveh) that was lived by, and was known for, its many cruel atrocities committed on those she conquered: amputating parts of bodies, impaling, beheading, burning, and piling up corpses. The thing that strengthened the sin in this city was described in the 4th verse: "Because of the multitude of the whoredoms of the wellfavoured harlot, the mistress of witchcrafts, that selleth nations through her whoredoms, and families through her witchcrafts." This nation became a terrible one because of the harlot and prostitution (sex, pornography). The relationships of the harlot were able to bring a city down to nothing.

The people forgot about the Lord and his ways, and they married out of the faith. The situation was so devastating that it brought Ezra to his knees: All of those months of traveling, bringing the people to Jerusalem, the place that belonged to them, the place of Peace only to see them disobey God. We cannot afford to disobey God in this day. Corporately speaking, we must become His house, and when Jezebel comes we must stand against that spirit. Don't allow her to teach or reign. If she doesn't teach, then she will not be able to produce. Stop the spirit that would *attempt* to place a *wedge* in the midst of God's house. Let the spirit of unity reign, flow, and most importantly lead.

The Remedy

Ezra 9:15
O Lord God of Israel, thou art righteous: for we remain yet escaped, as it is this day: behold, we are before thee in our trespasses: for we cannot stand before thee because of this.

Ezra 10:1
Now when Ezra had prayed, and when he had confessed, weeping and casting himself down before the house of God, there

assembled unto him out of Israel a very great congregation of
men and women and children: for the people wept very sore.

After Ezra prayed, confessed, cried, he cast himself down; the people also began to weep before the Lord. What happened was that the people did something that believers today feel is irrelevant: they repented. The Hebrew word for *repentance* is *shuwb* (shoob). It means "to turn back (hence, away) to turn again; to retreat." This word *shuwb* expresses the thought of turning or returning. The Greek word for *repentance* is *metanoeo* (met-an-o-eh'-o). It is made up of two words. The first word is *meta* (met-ah'), which means "after," implying change; the second word is *noieo* (noy-eh'-o), which means "to perceive, exercise the mind, observe, comprehend, heed." *Metanoeo* means "a change of mind."

The people in the book of Ezra that married into Jezebel heard the prayer of Ezra and cried out to the Lord; when they did that, it brought a time of repentance or a change of mind; they turned again, or returned, to the Lord. They returned to the principles of the Law. Many ministries make the mistake of developing so much that when they veer off from the will of God, they continue flowing in that state of disobedience and rebellion. The house is in three realms, remember? So when one walks away from truth or walks in rebellion, those three realms are affected. The first realm, which is the individual, is affected; the second realm, which is the local ministry, is affected; and because the first and second realms are affected, the third will be affected. The reason the third realm will be affected is because it will be hindered from being finished.

The prayer of Ezra initiated repentance and holy reform and that reform brought about a cleansing and that same type of reform is vital within a ministry when that ministry veers off. A prayer of reform will:

1. Cleanse the individual (first realm of the House)
2. Cleanse the local ministry (the framed House)
3. Cleanse the corporate body of Christ (the finished House)

Repentance means one has turned from sin and has made an about face. It is getting off the wrong path and onto the right path and going towards God. This process involves an inward turning from sin and

69

disposition to seek pardon and cleansing. Their repentance touched their wills in their hearts. This situation of the 10th chapter of Ezra calls for a time of repentance, and what is noticed throughout the message is that Ezra preaches to those who intermingled and conceived children.

> *Ezra 10:2*
> *And Shechaniah the son of Jehiel, one of the sons of Elam, answered and said unto Ezra, We have trespassed against our God, and have taken strange wives of the people of the land: yet now there is hope in Israel concerning this thing.*

Shechaniah, whose name means "the Lord dwells and resides," answered, "We have trespassed and taken strange wives." The repentance started by confessing or exposing the wrong that was done. Remember, the house starts as an individual thing (it starts with you the believer first) then moves into a framed or corporate local ministry. This was a situation that affected the whole house. Shechaniah, who represents leadership within the House of God, understood the call of reform and adhered to that call, and he along with others wept sore. When they wept sore, they reestablished covenantal relationship by promising to separate themselves. What we promise the Lord we must follow through because it will affect:

1. Us as individuals
2. Our families
3. Our Churches
4. Our future
5. Our destiny.

> *Ezra 10:3*
> *Now therefore let us make a covenant with our God to put away all the wives, and such as are born of them, according to the counsel of my lord, and of those that tremble at the commandment of our God; and let it be done according to the law.*

They put away:

1. All the wives (Jezebel)

2. Such are born of them (Jezebel's children; her seed)
3. Jezebel's teachings of (seduction, fornication)
4. That spirit which was able to kill the unity
5. The bondwomen (the one not of promise but of the flesh)
6. The strange women.

Ezra went into the chamber of Johanan, the son of Eliaship, and he did not eat any bread or drink any water (a fast). The reason for this action was that he was mourning because of the transgression of those who were carried away. The important thing that a people cannot do is:

1. Forget who they are
2. Forget whose they are
3. Forget why they are
4. Forget where they are going (their inheritance and destiny).

Those believers forgot their inheritance. They forgot that they were going up to Jerusalem (Peace of God), which is in Judah (the praises of God). Because they forgot, they became separated from the TRUTH and married strange women. Those strange women were women who caused them to come away from their teachings. This woman is Jezebel, her children, and most of all her teachings. There may be a great falling away. One might lose focus and begin to wonder after other gods; however, the remedy to that falling away will call for one thing, REPENTANCE. Change your mind; turn back towards God.

Chapter Seven

Seed Killers

Gen. 1:11-12
And God said, Let the earth bring forth grass, the herb yielding seed, and the fruit tree yielding fruit after his kind, whose seed is in itself, upon the earth: and it was so. And the earth brought forth grass, and herb yielding seed after his kind, and the tree yielding fruit, whose seed was in itself, after his kind: and God saw that it was good.

In building God a house, it is important to note that His house is one full of His seed. It is the Seed of God who produces more of God on planet Earth. Because we are the seed who are building God a house, the enemy attempts to kill the seed.

God is the God of all generations, and throughout Scripture, God created and caused what He created to reproduce. There are words that are expressed in Genesis 1:11-12, which are phrases that imply growth for the future and those words are *seed* and *after his kind*. Every type of life form in the garden was able to reproduce after its kind, including man.

Mal. 2:15
And did not he make one? Yet had he the residue of the spirit. And wherefore one? That he might seek a godly seed. Therefore take heed to your spirit, and let none deal treacherously against the wife of his youth.

In Malachi 2:15, God dealt with the marital situation; if there is a problem in marriage, that problem marriage can affect the seed produced from that union. This is why God instructed the prophet to tell the people to straighten out the marriage so that He might seek a godly "seed." Notice, the seed would be affected. Why Seed? Because seed is how life is reproduced.

In Genesis 22:17-18, Abraham was told that he is "Blessed" and that his seed will be multiplied like the stars and sand, was blessed; again the Lord uses the word *seed*. The seed will come forth out of Abraham and shall possess the portals or entrances of their enemies.

We are a seed created to reproduce seed so that God can be revealed through His people the seed. The seeds are created to bring about God's vision. The seed of Abraham is the seed and vision of God.

Let us look at Adam, for there is a truth that needs to be noticed. Adam was created a man, not a child. Look at the trees in the garden. First, God created the tree with seed in it. Then God commanded the tree to reproduce after its kind. Adam was created a man, but when Cain was born, Cain was a baby. The revelation of this is that God gave us the finished product first (Adam), then teaches us how a finished product comes about for it starts out as a seed. God always sees the finished product; however, He calls for the believer to mature into that finished or complete product. Seed is that which is to become God's finished product.

What is meant by the seed? The seed is that which causes or stimulates growth. It is that which becomes what is supposed to be. Seed in this teaching not only represents sons and daughters of God but also vision. What are seed killers? Seed killers are vision killers. They are murderers that attempt to extinguish a move and a generation that is born to bring about God's will.

What are seed killers? Seed killers are Vision killers that are religious men and women, spiritually pro-abortionist whose number one priority is to kill anything that speaks of the freshness of God. They are flesh hounds that seek other flesh to praise them. A seed killer functions as an oppressor, a false seed religion, or in a spirit of dictatorship. Those functioning's attempt to annihilate anything or anyone that houses God's possibility.

74

2 Kings 11:1-2
And when Athaliah the mother of Ahaziah saw that her son was
dead, she arose and destroyed all the seed royal. But Jehosheba,
the daughter of king Joram, sister of Ahaziah, took Joash the son
of Ahaziah, and stole him from among the king's sons which
were slain; and they hid him, even him and his nurse, in the
bedchamber from Athaliah, so that he was not slain.

In 2 Kings 11:1-2, there is a woman by the name of Athaliah. The name Athaliah is from the Hebrew word *Athalyah* (ath-al-yaw') which means "Jah has constrained." Athaliah has also been translated "Jehovah is strong, Jehovah suspends, distress or affliction of Jehovah." She was the daughter of Jezebel, and she inherited her mother's cruelty and ruthlessness. She married Jehoram, king of Judah, and influenced him and their son Ahaziah to reintroduce baal worship (a false seed religion). What is a false seed religion? It is a type of worship that is out of the confines of what God has sanctioned. It is total disobedience of Exodus 20:3, *"thou shalt have no other gods before me"* and also of Deuteronomy 6:5, *"And thou shalt love the Lord thy God with all thine heart, and with all thy soul, and with all thy might."* False seed religion is a false worship. False seed religion as it pertains to Athaliah is a ruling and controlling worship of what she sanctions and desires.

Athaliah's husband Jehoram died after only eight years of reigning as king. However, he was a seed and vision killer like his wife. Before Jehoram died, he had all of his brothers, who were the sons of Jehoshaphat, killed. His son Ahaziah, who died after only one year of reigning, succeeded him. It was after the death of Ahaziah that Athaliah, his mother, became Queen Mother of Judah, and it was during this time that she became a barbarian because she destroyed all of the Royal Seed. Remember, the seed also represents vision, and to kill the royal seed is to kill the vision of the Lord. Her complete focus and mission was to destroy the seed and vision.

Athaliah was a vision killer, a murderer who will kill anyone or anything who may pose as a threat to her program. Athaliah was a woman who had to be in control and would never be in subjection to anyone. She'll kill the spirit of Spiritual authority and Truth, and she's an anointing killer. During the time of her reign, she was a Barbarian, and she was the only woman in the Bible who ruled for as long as she did; She managed to rule Judah for six years (2 Kings 11:1-4).

When she began to reign, she had parts of the Temple dismantled to build a shrine to Baal. She took control of Judah and ordered the massacre of all her grandchildren. Athaliah killed all of the infants and sucklings that might have reigned after her for fear of competition. Her ultimate goal was to cut-off the house of David, but the house of David was God's promise to David.

In 2 Samuel, Chapter Seven, there were six promises that God gave to David. Of those six promises, three were to happen after David died. The first promise was an eternal seed: and your son will have a son and his son will have a son, etc. It eventually became the messianic line. No monarch had ever received a promise like that. The second promise was the eternal kingdom, which is an eternal sphere of rule. In essence, God said to David that I'm going to enter into a relationship with you and with your seed, and each King that sits on the throne in the messianic line. If they sin, I will bring in the other nations as chastening rods (2 Sam. 7:12-14). The third promise was that David's throne would be established forever. Athaliah wanted to do away with what God had promised David, and if she could have stomped out all of the seed, she would have. What does Athaliah represent prophetically? She represents the spirit of hindrance.

There are three types of spirits that are vision killers. The spirit of an oppressor, the spirit of a false seed religion, and the spirit of dictatorship. The spirit of an oppressor can crush the spirit of vision by harsh rule. The spirit of a false seed religion occurs when the spirit will release a type of idol worship, killing the spirit of true worship connected with vision. The spirit of dictatorship is a brutal one which uses that brutality to consolidate one's position. Herod the king was a dictator who attempted to kill the Royal Seed and Vision named Christ through the means of Herod's spirit of dictatorship.

Athaliah was a vision killer, but for every vision killer there is a seed protector or a vision protector. The seed protector in this situation is a woman named Jehoshabeath. Jehoshabeath was the daughter of King Jehoram of Judah. Athaliah was Jehoshabeath's stepmother. When Athaliah began to kill all of the royal seed, Jehoshabeath ran and got her infant nephew named Joash along with his nurse and hid them in a bedchamber. A bedchamber serves as a type of incubation and covering period. It keeps and nourishes infants who are not ready to live and breathe on their own. The bedchamber houses that which is infantile. Joash was the only surviving heir to the throne. Jehoshabeath hid Joash for six years. Athaliah reigned for six years. Six is the number of man (flesh), and all flesh must come to an end. In order for the reign of a false religion to come to an end, it will take an anointed leader that has the capability to bring people together. That person was Jehoiada.

> *2 Chr. 23:1-3*
> *And in the seventh year Jehoiada strengthened himself, and took the captains of hundreds, Azariah the son of Jeroham, and Ishmael the son of Jehohanan, and Azariah the son of Obed, and Maaseiah the son of Adaiah, and Elishaphat the son of Zichri, into covenant with him. And they went about in Judah, and gathered the Levites out of all the cities of Judah, and the chief of the fathers of Israel, and they came to Jerusalem. And all the congregation made a covenant with the king in the house of God. And he said unto them, Behold, the king's son shall reign, as the Lord hath said of the sons of David.*

Jehoiada was the high priest. The name Jehoiada means "Knowledge of God." The bible reads that Jehoiada strengthened himself or he took courage. The word *courage* means "the attitude of facing and dealing with anything recognized as dangerous, difficult, or painful; instead of withdrawing from that danger, one approaches that danger." This man of God had a yearning to impart the seed (vision) into the people even if his life was lost. What he did was take five men into covenant with him. Five is the number for authority. It represents the hand of the Lord. The "Five Fold Ministry" represents men and women of God who are able to set order within the body. Those five men were captains of 100-man platoons. They canvassed Judah and gathered Levites out of all the cities of Judah and the chief of the fathers of Israel. They all met in the city of Jerusalem. It is important to note that if the captains in the members had to canvass the area to look for the Levites, Priests, and head of the tribes, then this was a time when all of the offices were scattered. The church was separated at this point. Those five in covenant with the high priest ran and gathered all of the Levites out of Judah and all of the chief of the fathers from Israel.

2 Kings 11:5-6
And he commanded them, saying, This is the thing that ye shall do; A third part of you that enter in on the sabbath shall even be keepers of the watch of the king's house; [6] And a third part shall be at the gate of Sur; and a third part at the gate behind the guard: so shall ye keep the watch of the house, that it be not broken down.

Jehoiada divided the people into groups of threes. Three is the number for the third dimension. Whenever a spiritual disorder takes place within a church, it will take a third-dimensional walk in faith, understanding, and operation to root out that spirit. Because this was a situation that dealt with a false religion it had to be dealt with or that spirit would have impacted generations; it took third-dimensional truths and participation to get the rightful king back on the throne. One third of the people were the priests and Levites who were to watch the gates of the Temple when they came on duty during the Sabbath; this action represents constant prayer in the temple. Another third were to watch the king's house (Royal Palace); this action represents constant prayer over leadership and also a constant confessing of the word over the leadership so that vision remains clear and precise. As they watched over the king's palace, the Levites and priest had their swords drawn, which reveals walking with the word in the hands and in their hearts. It represents a time of consistent prayer so that vision does not get off track. The other third were to watch the Gate of the Foundation, which reveals prayer for the foundation and pillars and those in leadership positions of the house.

Joash the seed of vision came to the throne in the seventh year. Athaliah the vision and seed killer reigned for six years. This is the end of the sixth year; all flesh must come to an end. The enemy has had his time, but now it is the seventh year, the seventh day, the seventh hour. This is the time of the seventh which is the Day and Time of God being revealed. It is the day of the Seed maturing and becoming that vision.

Seven represents the day of God. Joash assumed the throne, and there was a ceremony. During this ceremony, Joash aligned the walls of the temple with his army. This action represents aligning the ministry with prayer and prayer warriors. We live in a time now when covering the ministry with prayer is vital. The enemy Athaliah heard what was happening and attempted to stop the ceremony at the temple, but the host of the army of Joash met her. It was an army of truth (the sword of the Spirit) that was there to cut away the false religious seed killer.

Athaliah, being restrained, began to yell "treason, treason." The false religion ran head first into the Truth, finding fault with the truth! The seed and vision was covered enough in prayer to take authority over the seed and vision killer and cast that spirit out. Joash had that spirit of false religion taken out of the temple and killed. Notice he did not have Athaliah killed inside the temple but outside so that the stench of that false religion and the seed of that religion would not remain in the house of God. Many times the aroma is just as bad as the spirit. The scapegoat was taken outside of Jerusalem.

Joash, the seed vision, was in order and flowing and also setting things in order, getting rid of false religion seed mixture and keeping the seed of Christ and vision whole and righteous. This action would have not been possible had it not been for someone who was willing to protect the seed and vision from the royal seed killer. Thank God for the many Jehoshabeaths and Jehoiada's that live in the presence of God within the kingdom of God.

Mary and Joseph were to save the most important seed of all, Jesus Christ. A lot of times, protecting the seed will bring what may seem like embarrassment from those who lack the Word, faith, and understanding. Herod wanted to kill all of the infant male seed so that he could annihilate the possibility of Christ. However, Mary and Joseph went to Egypt. Egypt represents the hiding of the seed until its time. *"For in the time of trouble he shall hide me in his pavilion: in the secret of his tabernacle shall he hide me; he shall set me up upon a rock"* (Ps 27:5).

It took spiritual strength for Jehoshabeath to put her life on the line and save the seed and vision; this represents the importance of hiding or protecting the seed. It took something for Shiphrah and Puah in Exodus 1:15-17 to put their lives on the line and not kill the Hebrew male babies for they covered the seed of vision. Mary and Joseph had to travel many miles by foot, placing themselves in much danger. The scripture also speaks of Ahimelech the priest who fed David with Shewbread (the Word of God). Ahimelech ended up losing his life along with many others so that the seed vision future King of Israel can live (1 Sam. 22:16). It takes a special person to overlook danger regardless of it staring him in the face in order that the will of God might be done. This represents a people who are willing to die for the cause of the Gospel and vision. How many people are placed on earth even in this day only to help birth seed? No notoriety, no fame or fortune, just people who were planted in the kingdom by God just to help for a specific season.

Jehoshabeath represents the importance of one hiding the seed. Jehoiada represents the importance of being willing to strengthen oneself in order to impart the seed vision into others who house possibility. The life of Shiphrah and Puah speaks of God creating those to help birth seed. We also must remember Hanna. The life of Hanna, the once barren mother of Samuel, reveals God's miraculous power taking effect in an individual that will teach us the importance of dedicating the seed. One must also think on the wife of Manoah, Samson's mother. For she reveals how important it is to live godly in order to produce a godly seed. For the angel told Manoah to make sure the wife does not drink from the vine or strong drink and also that she doesn't eat any unclean thing (Judges 13:13-14) because what she takes in can affect the seed she is bringing forth.

Mary and Joseph reveal to us that it may require leaving a particular place in order to protect the seed and that the seed must be protected even if one's life depended upon it.

There are seed killers and vision killers that roam the earth today. Their job is to kill the vision that God has placed in an individual. Whether those killers are an unanointed uncircumcised giant, or a fleshly egotistical self-proclaimed preacher, they are out to do the seed of God harm. However, just as there are giants in the land, there are also Shiphrah, Puah, Jehoshabeath, Mary, Joseph, and many more that were created by God to protect the seed of God from the seed and vision killers.

You are that seed, the part of God's vision that will impact hundreds and hundreds of lives. You are that seed that the oppressor, royal seed killer, and dictatorship mentality are looking to destroy, but just as there are seed killers that are looking to stop you, so are there seed birthers sent by God to help cover, nurture, and coach you. How many times have you, the believer, received an act or word from the Lord at the right time from someone whom you didn't know and have never seen again? How many times have you, the believer, pastor, etc., felt like giving up (aborting the seed) and vision God has placed in your heart?

But then, suddenly, a breakthrough and a breaking forth appear out of no where! That is because you are the Seed Royal, and though the King of Egypt (mentality), Athaliah, and Herod desire to kill you, they cannot because the Hand of the Lord is upon you, and it is this seed, you, the Seed Royal, that shall build and become the house of God!

Chapter Eight

The Baptism of the Local Ministry

Corporate ministry occurs when the local ministry functions as one. A corporate ministry requires a corporate anointing. This means that Christ must corporately anoint your local church. Now, many of you are asking why I added this chapter to this book. Well, here is the reason why. Upon my watching a movie one night, there was something in that movie that was said which was profound and true. In the movie the gentlemen said to some people who have suffered loss due to the closing of an old factory, "I am going to do something that politicians don't necessarily do and that is to tell you the truth." The people began to laugh and then listen. Keep in mind that is a group of people who suffered loss due to a factory closing. Strong-armed tactics caused the union to lose strength, and the factory was closed, and the people lost their jobs. So they wanted their jobs back; they wanted things like they used to be. The person then began to speak to the people, and he said, "No politician can reopen this factory or bring back the shipyard jobs or make your union strong again. No politician can make it the way it used to be because we are living in a new and more modern world." The local ministry which functions today must understand the importance of unity. It must also understand the importance of the corporate ministry moving forward in the Now, or in its proper time, because ministry and service unto the Lord will not be as it was. If the modern, technological, secular world is advancing, so must the corporate body also be advancing because church as a whole should be a leadership that is able to communicate and flow and be observed by its surroundings.

The local churches that plan on doing great things within the kingdom of God can never ever go back to the way things used to be even though it seems as though the times were better and easier. Why can the local church not go back to the way things were? The reason is because the times will not allow it.

Another time I watched a great man of God on television make an appeal to his listening audience. He was raising funds to renovate a historic site. The building, which is a monumental place, needed to be brought up to the standards for the 21st century meaning; the facility must be brought up to par. The place needed air conditioning, a modern PA system, and so on. Why did the man of God at this time suggest that the building be renovated? Because the leader realized that yesterday is gone, and it is time to manufacture or produce in the NOW of God.

Though we build buildings or build God a physical house, the corporate spiritual house must be intact. If the local ministry intends on corporately producing vision in the local assembly, community, and the world, then the local ministry, which consists of people from various backgrounds and walks of life, can no longer operate as a group or number of people but must become "One" or "Corporate." The ministry must corporately be "Baptized" into the spiritual body and person of Christ. In regards to the local ministry, it will require a baptism within the local ministry.

Many in ministry, especially those who have been in ministry for a long time, will have a hard time releasing yesterday in order to function and produce in the today. The old mentality and ways must be dead and buried corporately.

1 Cor. 10:1-2
Moreover, brethren, I would not that ye should be ignorant, how that all our fathers were under the cloud, and all passed through the sea; And were all baptized unto Moses in the cloud and in the sea;

Acts 7:38
This is he, that was in the church in the wilderness with the angel which spake to him in the mount Sina, and with our fathers: who received the lively oracles to give unto us:

What is the Baptism of the Local Ministry? First we must look at baptism as a whole. According to Acts 7:38, the Children of Israel (the Church) was in the wilderness and baptized unto Moses (a type of Christ) for Moses was the mediator of the Old Covenant. Today you and I are baptized into the Lord Jesus Christ, the Mediator of the New Covenant. When the Children of Israel were at the Red Sea, Pharaoh followed behind them; however, the Red Sea swallowed the army of Pharaoh. The water served as deliverance to the Children of Israel. As we are baptized into Christ, sin is swallowed up and it has dominion over us no more (Romans 6:14).

The Greek word for *baptize* is *baptizo* (bap-tid'-zo), which means "to make whelmed or fully wet." The root word for *baptize* is *bapto,* which means "to cover wholly with fluid." So, when one is baptized he or she is covered fully with fluid. When the local ministry is baptized into the body of the Lord Jesus we are covered fully with the Lord Jesus Christ, for we are baptized into Him. Is it possible for a complete local church to be baptized? Well, let me ask you, were not the Children of Israel baptized unto Moses? According to 1st Corinthians 10:1-2, absolutely. There are three things that took place when the Children of Israel went into the Red Sea:

1. They went down in the water of the Red Sea. This represents the death.
2. They walked across the floor of the Red Sea. This represents the burial.
3. They came up from the Red Sea. This represents the resurrection.

This shows a type of baptism into or unto Moses.

What then is the baptism of the Local Ministry? The baptism of the Local Ministry is "the spiritual full immersion of the local corporate ministry into the Lord Jesus Christ." It is the baptism of our minds since they die only to be buried and then are resurrected into "one mind" which is the mind of Christ (Phil. 2:5). In the baptism of the local ministry, one's mentality must die in order that we may gain a corporate mentality of Christ. As we build God's physical house, our mentality must become corporate like His House. A local ministry cannot return to a mentality of separatism but must be changed into a corporate baptized mind of Christ. A baptized corporate mind will never return to the former things, for it is the former things that can kill a flow. The baptized local ministry must be smarter and use what is between their ears, which is the mind of Christ.

> *Gal. 2:20*
> *I am crucified with Christ: nevertheless I live; yet not I, but Christ liveth in me: and the life which I now live in the flesh I live by the faith of the Son of God, who loved me, and gave himself for me.*

Let us notice the word *crucified* in Galatians 2:20. It is the Greek word *sustauroo* (soos-tow-ro'-o). This word is a perfect tense verb, meaning it is an action that is completed in the past with ongoing results in the present. Notice also the "I am," for in the present tense meaning it should read, "I am 'being' crucified with Christ." We are crucified in three realms; we have been, are being, and shall be crucified. The old man was crucified and died. Nevertheless I live; yet not I, but now that I am being crucified; Christ is now living in me and through me, for the life that I live now I live by the faith of the Son of God. That life is the life of the Son of God, which flows throughout corporate ministry. It is a constant reminder of the crucifixion since the body is crucified along with the mind; therefore, it is important to lose your mind, "*For who hath known the mind of the Lord, that he may instruct him? But we have the mind of Christ*" (1 Cor. 2:16).

How do we walk in that corporate Baptism? It requires a people to lose their minds and become "His" (Christ's) mind. Walking in corporate baptism requires a burial of an old identity and mentality. We walk in corporate baptism by walking as One man fully immersed in Christ with a fresh and renewed outlook on ministry. It is a pace which leads the local church into functioning in a realm that is unhindered.

> *Hosea 4:6*
> *My people are destroyed for lack of knowledge:*

There are a few words to be noticed in Hosea 4:6. The word *destroyed* is the Hebrew word *damah* (daw-maw) and means "to be dumb or silent; hence to fail or perish." The word *lack* is the Hebrew word *beliy* (bel-ee'); the root word means "decaying;" the word itself means "failure," so the word *lack* means "a decaying failure." Finally, the word *knowledge* is the Hebrew word *da'ath* (dah'-ath); the root word means "to know to ascertain by seeing." What this scripture is saying is, "My people are dumb or silent and they fail or perish because of their decaying failure to know or ascertain by seeing." A local ministry can become destroyed for refusing to know who they are or refusing to become baptized (immersed) into Christ corporately.

1. The old individual mind is killed - death (yesterdays way of doing things)
2. The old individual mind is buried – burial (because it's a dead thing, a dead issue). Why is the old mind and old dead issues buried? To get rid of the odor!
3. The new corporate mind (mind of Christ) is resurrected – resurrection (Fresh anointing and fresh oil).

Returning to something that is dead can be detrimental. Many times, especially in ministry, the very thing that the church misses is the thing that it longs for. It is that thing that has killed a move in the first place. Many desire to return to where the church of old has left off; however, that mentality needs to be buried. Where we left off is gone and will never ever be the same. We want to go back to a memory of specific style more so than a wholesome fresh move of God. Some have the "Well I'm from the old school" attitude. What you are saying is that you graduated from an era and refuse to grow or to become re-taught or baptized into His person today. This is the day that the Lord has made, and because He has made this day, He expects His baptized corporate body to walk in this day, for we are baptized into a higher realm of service in Christ.

Rom 8:19
For the earnest expectation of the creature waiteth for the manifestation of the sons of God.

The Baptized Local Ministry must take its rightful place in ministry and also in the community. That rightful place is one of leadership. The ministry of Christ always flows in the now and operates at a level which causes others to desire and follow. It is a ministry that never flows in the thought pattern of what it was, but always in the pattern of who and what it represents in the present. If we are ministers of Christ, then we must flow like Christ flows. The local churches as a whole must stand in the gap, for it is where the ministry is supposed to be, for He (Christ) is no longer looking for a man but a corporate Son.

Ezekiel 22:30
"And I sought for a man among them, that should make up the hedge, and stand in the gap before me for the land, that I should not destroy it: but I found none."

I sought for a man and that man prophetically speaking is the corporate son who needs to get into his proper place. If the gifted men of God would take their rightful place, it would produce a flow of divine order, which in turn would produce a flow of God. The morale of the people is down because there is nothing new. We're operating from an old anointing and an old flow or old wine. Jesus prayed in Matthew 6:11 that we would receive bread daily; however, there is no freshness, which means that the bread is stale. We are not receiving new bread because there is an opening or a gap. A gap that should not be gives place for the enemy, and God will withhold the rain and the bread. We have neither rain nor bread; however, there is a gap. Let corporately baptized people function with His mind, which will bring about a new flow of order.

The mentality of a corporate baptism is one of excellence; the word *excellent* is the Hebrew word *yether* (yeh'-ther) which means "an overhanging; it implies excess, superiority." The root word is the Hebrew word *yathar* (yaw-thar), which means "to jut over or exceed; it implies to excel." When we speak of excellence we speak of excess, superiority, and excelling. What are we excelling in? We are to excel in PERFECTION! Corporate people of baptism are people who go beyond the limit, for they are "unlimited" in their service unto the Lord. The baptized local ministry is one corporate, unlimited man functioning and pursuing the purpose and ministry of the kingdom of God. It is a people who have understands the "thy will be done on earth as it is in heaven" passage.

The spirit of excellence is the spirit of excelling to be perfect or professional in all areas of ministry and personal lives. Excellence is an attitude of professionalism and perfection both spiritually and physically. It is an attitude that says, "I offer unto God the very best that I can give." One's attitude of excellence determines one's altitude (how high you go or how successful you become). If ministries are determined to become the very house and habitation of God, then they must be determined also to become His excellence. God's Spirit is one of excellence; He gives His children the very best that He had and has to offer. A corporate baptized local ministry has the mentality to offer up or function in the service of excellence, which is an attitude of giving the very best that we have to offer.

> *Jer. 18:4-6*
> *And the vessel that he made of clay was marred in the hand of the potter: so he made it again another vessel, as seemed good to the potter to make it. Then the word of the Lord came to me, saying, O house of Israel, cannot I do with you as this potter? saith the Lord. Behold, as the clay is in the potter's hand, so are ye in mine hand, O house of Israel.*

Remember what was stated at the beginning of this chapter, that *"Corporate ministry requires a corporate anointing,"* and this means that Christ must corporately anoint your local church. The anointing of God will only be housed in vessels of excellence; it will not rest in just anything. The anointing is spiritual oil that flows upon believers equipping them to do what God has called them into. Corporately the anointing will flow upon and be housed in a people. In Jeremiah 18:4-6 the vessels are believers that were shaped according to what the Father had in His mind, meaning that God fashioned you into what He desired. Corporately God is fashioning the local ministry into what He desires and as the Father makes the vessels ready for His corporate oil; He will fix those corporate vessels so that they can hold the oil. From here on out, realize that your local ministry must be baptized corporately so that all will speak and believe the same thing. Secondly the baptized ministry must give God the very best and also function in that way corporately for corporate excellence is an attitude that determines the corporate ministries altitude. The baptism of the local ministry occurs when a local church is submerged into Christ's anointing and comes up out of that anointing as One Corporate Man, not a divided people.

How do we get to that place in God and become that local baptized ministry? We are a prepared Body who houses the very fullness of Him. We must get the understanding of this revelation. The baptism of the local ministry will only come through prayer and pushing. Once this is understood, the local ministry can walk in the full benefits of the corporate local baptism, which is a full manifestation of unlimited power for the church. We get to the place in God to become that local baptized ministry through prayer and pushing, which operates like faith and works. You can't have one without the other. Faith without works is dead; prayer without pushing is dead, useless. What is meant by pray and push?

P	Prepared by Him
R	Reflection of Him
A	Abounding through Him
Y	Yearning for more of Him

P	Prayer for the manifestation
U	Unceasingly – Don't stop praying
S	Seize – seize the manifestation
H	Habitation – we live in the manifestation

P means we are prepared by Him. **R** means we become the reflection of Him. **A** means we are abounding through Him. **Y** means through prayer we yearn for more of Him. **P** in push means constant prayer for the manifestation of Him. **U** means unceasingly prayer; in other words, don't stop praying. **S** means to seize that manifestation, and **H** means habitation whereby we live in that manifestation.

Chapter Nine

Arise!

The Lord is getting ready to close up the breaches. He is going to cause the ruins in your life to be built as they were destined to be in the mind of God before there was even a beginning. God is restoring the focus of those who have lost that focus. He is leading us from Babylon, a time of confusion, into Jerusalem, Judah, which is that place of peace and praise. Who are those that He is bringing? He is bringing a people who are called by His name (2 Chr 7:14).

Arise Cyrus

The Lord is calling for Cyrus the gentile king, the one voted the least likely to succeed. He is calling for Cyrus the one who does not fit the protocol of whom man thinks should lead. He is calling for Cyrus, the one who represents the last overlooked son of Jessie. Arise, for the Lord is sending Samuel the prophet down to the house of Jessie to anoint a king whom God has chosen. Cyrus represents those who were looked over by men, who lacked vision, yet Cyrus is the one that God called.

The Father is calling for Noah, the one who will build God a house in the midst of a community that lacks vision and therefore does not understand why. The non-believers will call the vision foolish; however, you, Noah, will stay focused because of the call of God, which is to build Him a house.

The Church of God is coming into order and alignment. We are coming into alignment with our finances, families, and inheritance. Nothing is too good for the purpose and ministry of God. The project is funded, and the masons are ready to enclose the house with prayer. The carpenters (teachers) are getting into position to frame and build the ministry. There is plenty of Meat (which is the will of God) to be eaten, for the will of God is flowing. There is drink of a new wine because the wine skins have been revived and are ready to house the drink of the Lord. The oil of the Lord is flowing in order; it is flowing from the head of the church, which is Christ, down through the leadership of the local ministry.

We are coming into alignment because we realize that it is the seventh day, the Day of God. We are building the House. First the individual stage, then the local ministry stage, and finally the corporate body. As we become built, we dance and shout about what God has done and is doing. It's time to dance, to let your enemies know that God is causing us to ARISE. It's time to dance because God has fixed and repaired us and has taken us out of the city of confusion into the city of blessing.

The Adversary is defeated. The categorization of the world and those in the church who are non-believers (lack faith) is unnoticed as we pursue the will of God. There is a new or fresh order within Leadership. It is the order of the Lord that is going forth.
Arise Haggai and Zechariah

Arise Haggai and Zechariah, for the Lord is calling for you. Arise; get up, for you will be anointed enough to walk into visions that had been put aside. You will be able to help ministries resurrect vision; you will be able to help ministries reestablish the spirit of prayer by pulling the altar out of the rubble and setting it on its base. All that has held up will be released through your ministry.

Arise Ezra

Arise, Ezra, for the Lord is calling for you. Years have transpired, and it has been dead in our churches and cities for a long time. It felt as though the prophetic was silent, but the Lord is speaking, and what He is speaking is in the now, the right now. Arise, Ezra, and begin to walk in your called office of the prophetic; the spirit of Ezra is upon many of you that are reading. You are anointed to write prophetically and instruct in the things of God. Because you will be able to write in the prophetic, you will also walk in the favor of the Lord. The favor of the Lord will cause you to walk in the favor of man. As previously stated, scribes have the spirit of the eagle. The spirit of the eagle is the spirit of the prophet. You will function as the fingers of the Holy Spirit, and you shall be lead of the spirit, and what is written through you shall be inscribed upon the hearts that receive.

As Ezra writes, it will produce not only blessing and impregnation but also at times will produce confession and repentance. Your anointed writings will cause many to cry out to the Lord. The writings will break many generational curses, and also curses that have hovered over ministries for years. Your writings will consist of holy reform, which will bring about cleansing.

Arise Jehoshabeath and Jehoiada

Arise, Jehoshabeath and Jehoiada; the Lord is calling for you. For you will stand against those who stand against spiritual authority. You will not be afraid to cover those who house purpose. You will take courage and have the attitude of facing and dealing with anything recognized as dangerous, difficult, or painful, and instead of withdrawing from that danger, you will approach that danger without fear of your own life. Not only will you hide the seed which houses purpose, but you will also encourage the people to follow the vision.

Arise, you, the believer, the local ministry and corporate body

Arise believers; the Lord is calling for you. It is time for the church as a whole to take its rightful place here on earth. It's time for us to be divided no longer but to become baptized together that we may become one man, a corporate man who walks through the community, causing God Himself to have dominion. Arise and be baptized into the corporate mentality of excellence. It is time for the church to excel in perfection whereby it allows us to function under the anointing, doing limitless impossibilities for the kingdom of God. In this realm we will understand Mathew 6:10, *"Thy kingdom come. Thy will be done in earth, as it is in heaven."*

This is the season of prayer and pushing. Once we understand that the principle of success within ministry is prayer and pushing, then we will have built the house that Father God is calling for.

I release all those who house ministries that have been referred to in this book. I call you to arise now. I declare that the house that the father is calling for shall be built in all three realms and that you, my brothers and sisters, shall be those vessels that have been shaped by God and made to house the anointing, which is released within the kingdom at this hour. For it is at this hour that the Father is calling for his house to be built and for the house to come forth in power and might. Again I say, Arise!

Dr. Robert L Robinson

Books by Dr. Robinson

Can these bones live?
Gives specific prophetic instructions on how
the ministry can be the ministry God are calling forth

The Authority of the Kingdom
The kingdom of God is here on earth within
the believer and because of this position the believers
must seek the kingdom in order to know more of and
understand the kingdom.

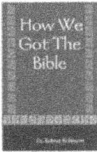

How we got the Bible w/workbook
This book gives information concerning the history
and makeup of the Bible. It deals with the many testing
that were done in order to prove its authenticity. Comes with a workbook

Build Me a House
based on a teaching coming from the Old Testament book Ezra. This writing
serves as a motivational prophetic Word to local churches encouraging them
to complete the vision

Hebrews Chapter Nine "The Interpretation"
A teaching based on Hebrews chapter nine
which deals with the Tabernacle of Moses.

The Ministry of the Tabernacle w/workbook
Book based on the Tabernacle of Moses

Build Me A House Correspondence Course
Build Me A House Correspondence Course is both a course and study guide
based on Dr. Robinson's book entitled "Build Me A House." The course is
based upon the book Ezra deals with church government and order.

A Sevenfold Purpose

A Sevenfold Purpose is the revealing of the will of God to His church as it pertains to alignment and order. The seven part plan is noted in the six days of creation leading into the seventh day.

Revelation, The Book w/workbook

Revelation , The Book is a commentary on the Book of Revelations which is the last prophetical book in the Bible

An Appointed Time

An Appointed Time is a set time, and This book prophetically deals with how the body of Christ must handle the appointed time allotted them.

Words Defined Prophetically

A book containing a selection of Biblical, Hebrew and Greek words detailing information concerning their meaning

Lessons I've Learned

This book is a compilation of bible studies taught by Dr. Robinson at a time when House of Manna Ministries in its inception stage

A Survey of the Old Testament w/ workbook

This book gives information pertaining to the Old Testament. A survey of the Old Testament deals with the History of Israel, their Kings, prophets, priests and ordinances. Book includes the workbook.

The Numbers Revealed

Throughout Scripture, numbers are used in order to reveal the hidden things of God. Through numbers God will release those things that are concealed.

The Necessity For Leadership
This book looks at leadership throughout the bible
and deals with the importance of leaders aligning to God's order.

His Praise
In the King James Version (KJV) bible, the word praise is mentioned
over one hundred and sixty times. However, in the original Hebrew,
each praise words denotes a different meaning and action.

A Time to Work
This book is a word from the Lord that relates to
a period when God will release an anointing for
seed time and harvest

A Sevenfold Purpose Workbook
The Workbook to A Sevenfold Purpose

Jude's Letter
This is a writing based upon the book of Jude.   In it you will find that Jude
not only wrote to his generation, but his writings are prophetic
which allowed for those writings to also speak to this generation.

The Four Anointings
A prophetical writing on the four rivers
noted in Genesis chapter 3

Be Free
Words of encouragement coming from both Pastor Glenda
and Apostle Robinson

What are you Birthing?
Zacharias was an old man who was called and used
by God to birth a son that was very important to the kingdom.
You are not old, you just need to find your way.

Vision "The Pattern"
Vision is a book that goes into detail on how to manifest vision

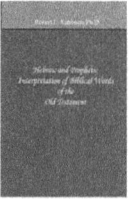

Hebraic and Prophetic Interpretation of Biblical Words of the Old Testament
A compilation of word definitions and meanings from biblical words in the Old Testament.

Feasts of the Lord
The Feasts of the Lord is a prophetic look at the
Old Testament Feast Days

For information on other material by Dr. Robert Robinson Please contact

Dr. Robert L Robinson Ministries
PO Box 10106
Cranston, RI 02910

www.robertrobinsonministries.org

www.ingramcontent.com/pod-product-compliance
Lightning Source LLC
Chambersburg PA
CBHW060131050426
42448CB00010B/2075